W9-ARW-691

Daily 6-Trait Writing GRADE 2

Editorial Development: Barbara Allman
Leslie Sorg
Andrea Weiss
Copy Editing: Cathy Harber
Art Direction: Cheryl Puckett
Cover Design: Liliana Potigian
Illustrators: Ann Iosa
Mary Rojas
Design/Production: Carolina Caird

EMC 6022

Evan-Moor®
EDUCATIONAL PUBLISHERS
Helping Children Learn since 1979

Congratulations on your purchase of some of the finest teaching materials in the world.

Correlated
to State Standards

For information about other Evan-Moor products, call 1-800-777-4362, fax 1-800-777-4332, or visit our Web site, www.evan-moor.com. Entire contents © 2008 EVAN-MOOR CORP. 18 Lower Ragsdale Drive, Monterey, CA 93940-5746. Printed in USA.

Visit *teaching-standards.com* to view a correlation of this book's activities to your state's standards. This is a free service.

CPSIA: Media Lithographics, 6080 Triangle Drive, City of Commerce, CA USA. 90040 [7/2010]

Contents

How to Use This Book

Daily 6-Trait Writing contains 25 weeks of mini-lessons divided into five units. Each unit provides five weeks of scaffolded instruction focused on one of the following traits: **Ideas, Organization, Word Choice, Sentence Fluency,** and **Voice.** (See pages 6–9 for more information about each of these, as well as the sixth trait, **Conventions**.) You may wish to teach each entire unit in consecutive order, or pick and choose the lessons within the unit.

Each week of *Daily 6-Trait Writing* focuses on a specific skill within the primary trait, as well as one Convention skill. The weeks follow a consistent five-day format, making *Daily 6-Trait Writing* easy to use.

Teacher Overview Pages

Trait Skill

A specific writing skill for each trait is targeted.

Reduced Pages

Reduced student pages provide sample answers.

Convention Skill

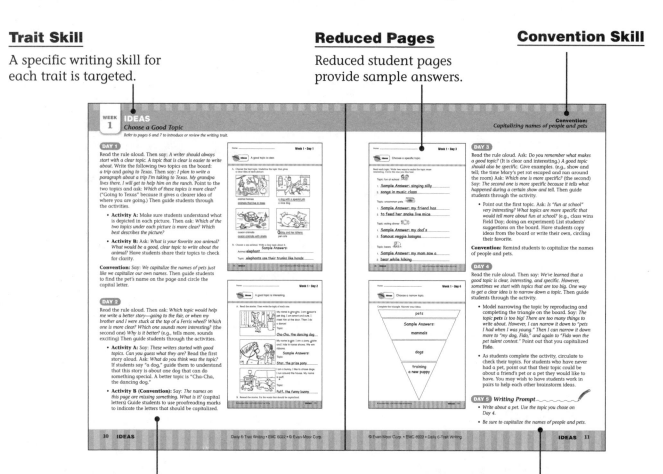

Lesson Plans

Use the lesson plans to teach the trait and Convention skills and guide students through the activities on Days 1–4. The plans are structured to enable you to differentiate and tailor lessons for your own class, but still provide the explanation and support you need. You may choose to have students complete the activities as a class, in small groups, or independently.

Day 5 Writing Prompt

Give your students the writing prompt to apply the trait and Convention skills in their own writing. Provide students with paper, or use the page provided for Day 5 in the student practice book. You may also wish to expand the writing prompt into a more fully developed assignment that takes students through the writing process.

Student Activity Pages

Trait and Rule (Skill Summary)

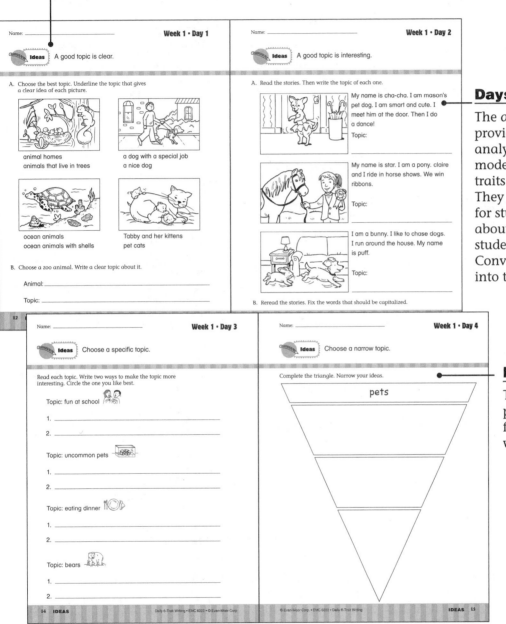

Days 1–3 Activities

The activities on Days 1–3 provide models for students to analyze, revise, or add to. These models expose students to the traits in many forms of writing. They also provide opportunities for students to think critically about writing, enhancing students' own proficiency. The Convention skill is integrated into the activities.

Day 4 Activity

The Day 4 activity provides a prewriting form for the Day 5 writing prompt.

Ways to Use

There are many ways to integrate *Daily 6-Trait Writing* into your classroom:

- Teach the lessons trait by trait.
- Target and practice specific skills students need help with.
- Use the lessons to enhance writing workshops.
- Incorporate the lessons into your other writing programs.

Use these ideas to introduce or review the trait at the beginning of each unit.

Ideas

Explain to students that good writing starts with good ideas.

Say: *A good idea is clear, interesting, and original. It makes the reader say, "Wow!" or "I never would have thought of that!" Without good ideas, your writing would not have much of a point. Your reader would be bored!*

Organization

Explain to students that good writing is organized in a way that helps the reader understand the information and follow what the writer is saying.

Say: *The organization of your writing is what holds everything together. It puts your ideas in an order that makes sense, and it gives your writing a strong beginning, middle, and end. When your writing is not organized, your reader can grow confused and lose interest.*

Word Choice

Explain to students that good writers choose their words carefully in order to get their ideas across.

Say: *When you write, choose just the right words and use them correctly. Make them fun and interesting so they help your readers "see" what you are talking about. Try not to use the same words over and over again. If you don't choose your words carefully, your reader may not understand what you're trying to say.*

Sentence Fluency

Explain to students that good writers make their writing flow by using different kinds of sentences.

Say: *You want your writing to be easy to read and follow. It should flow so smoothly and sound so interesting that people want to read it aloud! When your sentences don't flow, your writing sounds choppy and flat. Your reader would not want to read it aloud.*

Voice

Explain to students that when they write, their personality, or who they are, should shine through.

Say: *You want your writing to sound like you, and no one else! When you write, you show who you are through words. No matter what type of writing you do, always make sure it sounds like you. Otherwise, your reader may not care about what you have to say. In fact, your reader may not even know who wrote it!*

Conventions

Explain to students that good writers follow all the rules, or conventions, of writing, so their readers can easily read and understand the writing.

Say: *Using correct grammar, spelling, and punctuation when you write is important. When you don't follow the rules, your reader can become lost or confused. He or she may not know where one idea starts and another begins.*

Using the Rubric

Use the rubric on pages 8 and 9 to evaluate and assess your students' skill acquisition.

- Each week, evaluate the student responses to the Day 5 writing prompt using the criteria that correspond to the skills taught that week.

- For review weeks, use all the trait criteria to assess students' understanding of that trait as a whole.

- Use the entire set of criteria to occasionally assess students' writing across the traits.

- In student- and parent-teacher conferences, use the rubric to accurately and clearly explain what a student does well in writing, as well as what he or she needs to improve.

Use this scoring rubric, based on the six-traits writing model, to assess your students' writing.

Scoring Rubric

Student's Name _____

	1	2	3	4	Score
Ideas	• Has few, if any, original ideas. • Lacks or has a poorly developed topic; lacks a topic sentence. • Has few, if any, details. • Has little or no focus.	• Has some original ideas. • Has a minimally developed topic; may or may not have a topic sentence. • Some details are present. • Focus strays.	• Has original ideas. • Has a fairly well-developed topic stated in a topic sentence. • Has some details that support the topic. • Generally maintains focus.	• Has original ideas that tie in with each other. • Has a fully developed topic and a clear topic sentence that expresses the main idea. • Has carefully selected, interesting details that support the topic. • Maintains focus throughout.	
Organization	• Has little or no organization; lacks coherence. • Lacks a beginning, middle, and/or end. • Is difficult to follow. • Has no order words or phrases.	• Some organization is present. • Has a beginning, middle, and end, but may be unclear. • Is difficult to follow at times. • Has few or ineffective order words and/or phrases.	• Has logical organization. • Has a beginning, middle, and end. • Is fairly easy to follow. • Has order words and/or phrases.	• Has clear and logical organization. • Has a complete beginning, middle, and end. • Is very easy to follow. • Has appropriate order words and/or phrases.	
Word Choice	• Has a limited range of words. • Words are not appropriate for purpose and audience. • Words are used incorrectly. • Word choice shows little thought and precision.	• Uses passive verbs. • Uses few modifiers. • Some words may not be appropriate for the audience and purpose. • A few words are used incorrectly. • Word choice includes some clichés and "tired" words.	• Uses some strong verbs. • Uses some modifiers. • Words are mostly appropriate for the audience and purpose. • Words are used correctly but do not enhance the writing. • Words show thought and precision; clichés and "tired" words are avoided.	• Has many strong verbs. • Has many strong modifiers. • Words are consistently appropriate for audience and purpose. • Words are used correctly and enhance the writing. • Word choice is thoughtful and precise and includes some figurative language.	
Sentence Fluency	• Does not write complete sentences. • Writes only run-on or rambling sentences. • Has no variation in sentence structures and lengths. • Has no variation in sentence beginnings. • Has no cadence or flow in sentences.	• Has some incomplete sentences. • Has some run-on or rambling sentences. • Has little variation in sentence structures and lengths. • Has little variation in sentence beginnings. • Sentences flow somewhat.	• Has 1 or 2 incomplete sentences. • Has 1 or 2 run-on or rambling sentences. • Has some variation in sentence structures and lengths. • Has some variation in sentence beginnings. • Sentences flow fairly naturally.	• Has complete sentences. • Has no run-on or rambling sentences. • Varied sentence structures and lengths contribute to the rhythm of the writing. • Varied sentence beginnings contribute to the flow of the writing. • Sentences flow naturally.	
Voice	• Writing is neither expressive nor engaging. • Voice is not appropriate for the purpose, audience, topic, and/or genre. • Little evidence of an individual voice.	• Writing has some expression. • Voice is generally appropriate for the purpose, audience, topic, and/or genre. • Voice comes and goes.	• Writing is expressive and somewhat engaging. • Voice is appropriate for the purpose, audience, topic, and/or genre. • The voice is unique.	• Writing is very expressive and engaging. • Voice is consistently appropriate for the purpose, audience, topic, and/or genre. • The voice is unique, honest, and passionate.	
Conventions	• Has multiple errors in grammar, punctuation, and mechanics. • Poor handwriting and/or presentation makes the writing hard to read. • Illustrations, if present, do not accurately portray the main idea.	• Has some errors in grammar, punctuation, and mechanics. • Handwriting and/or presentation is fairly clear. • Illustrations, if present, portray the main idea but do not enhance it.	• Has few errors in grammar, punctuation, and mechanics. • Handwriting and/or presentation is clear. • Illustrations, if present, accurately portray the main idea and enhance it somewhat.	• Has minimal errors in grammar, punctuation, and mechanics. • Handwriting and/or presentation of the piece is attractive and easy to read. • Illustrations, if present, enhance the main idea significantly.	
				TOTAL	

Use this scoring rubric, based on the six-traits writing model, to assess your students' writing.

Scoring Rubric

Student's Name _____

	1	2	3	4	Score
Ideas	• Has few, if any, original ideas. • Lacks or has a poorly developed topic; lacks a topic sentence. • Has few, if any, details. • Has little or no focus.	• Has some original ideas. • Has a minimally developed topic; may or may not have a topic sentence. • Some details are present. • Focus strays.	• Has original ideas. • Has a fairly well-developed topic stated in a topic sentence. • Has some details that support the topic. • Generally maintains focus.	• Has original ideas that tie in with each other. • Has a fully developed topic and a clear topic sentence that expresses the main idea. • Has carefully selected, interesting details that support the topic. • Maintains focus throughout.	
Organization	• Has little or no organization; lacks coherence. • Lacks a beginning, middle, and/or end. • Is difficult to follow. • Has no order words or phrases.	• Some organization is present. • Has a beginning, middle, and end, but may be unclear. • Is difficult to follow at times. • Has few or ineffective order words and/or phrases.	• Has logical organization. • Has a beginning, middle, and end. • Is fairly easy to follow. • Has order words and/or phrases.	• Has clear and logical organization. • Has a complete beginning, middle, and end. • Is very easy to follow. • Has appropriate order words and/or phrases.	
Word Choice	• Has a limited range of words. • Words are not appropriate for purpose and audience. • Words are used incorrectly. • Word choice shows little thought and precision.	• Uses passive verbs. • Uses few modifiers. • Some words may not be appropriate for the audience and purpose. • A few words are used incorrectly. • Word choice includes some clichés and "tired" words.	• Uses some strong verbs. • Uses some modifiers. • Words are mostly appropriate for the audience and purpose. • Words are used correctly but do not enhance the writing. • Words show thought and precision; clichés and "tired" words are avoided.	• Has many strong verbs. • Has many strong modifiers. • Words are consistently appropriate for audience and purpose. • Words are used correctly and enhance the writing. • Word choice is thoughtful and precise and includes some figurative language.	

Sentence Fluency	• Does not write complete sentences. • Writes only run-on or rambling sentences. • Has no variation in sentence structures and lengths. • Has no variation in sentence beginnings. • Has no cadence or flow in sentences.	• Has some incomplete sentences. • Has some run-on or rambling sentences. • Has little variation in sentence structures and lengths. • Has little variation in sentence beginnings. • Sentences flow somewhat.	• Has 1 or 2 incomplete sentences. • Has 1 or 2 run-on or rambling sentences. • Has some variation in sentence structures and lengths. • Has some variation in sentence beginnings. • Sentences flow fairly naturally.	• Has complete sentences. • Has no run-on or rambling sentences. • Varied sentence structures and lengths contribute to the rhythm of the writing. • Varied sentence beginnings contribute to the flow of the writing. • Sentences flow naturally.
Voice	• Writing is neither expressive nor engaging. • Voice is not appropriate for the purpose, audience, topic, and/or genre. • Little evidence of an individual voice.	• Writing has some expression. • Voice is generally appropriate for the purpose, audience, topic, and/or genre. • Voice comes and goes.	• Writing is expressive and somewhat engaging. • Voice is appropriate for the purpose, audience, topic, and/or genre. • The voice is unique.	• Writing is very expressive and engaging. • Voice is consistently appropriate for the purpose, audience, topic, and/or genre. • The voice is unique, honest, and passionate.
Conventions	• Has multiple errors in grammar, punctuation, and mechanics. • Poor handwriting and/or presentation makes the writing hard to read. • Illustrations, if present, do not accurately portray the main idea.	• Has some errors in grammar, punctuation, and mechanics. • Handwriting and/or presentation is fairly clear. • Illustrations, if present, portray the main idea but do not enhance it.	• Has few errors in grammar, punctuation, and mechanics. • Handwriting and/or presentation is clear. • Illustrations, if present, accurately portray the main idea and enhance it somewhat.	• Has minimal errors in grammar, punctuation, and mechanics. • Handwriting and/or presentation of the piece is attractive and easy to read. • Illustrations, if present, enhance the main idea significantly.

TOTAL

DAY 1

Read the rule aloud. Then say: *A writer should always start with a clear topic. A topic that is clear is easier to write about.* Write the following two topics on the board: *a trip* and *going to Texas.* Then say: *I plan to write a paragraph about a trip I'm taking to Texas. My grandpa lives there. I will get to help him on the ranch.* Point to the two topics and ask: *Which of these topics is more clear?* ("Going to Texas" because it gives a clearer idea of where you are going.) Then guide students through the activities.

- **Activity A:** Make sure students understand what is depicted in each picture. Then ask: *Which of the two topics under each picture is more clear? Which best describes the picture?*

- **Activity B:** Ask: *What is your favorite zoo animal? What would be a good, clear topic to write about the animal?* Have students share their topics to check for clarity.

Convention: Say: *We capitalize the names of pets just like we capitalize our own names.* Then guide students to find the pet's name on the page and circle the capital letter.

DAY 2

Read the rule aloud. Then ask: *Which topic would help me write a better story—going to the fair, or when my brother and I were stuck at the top of a Ferris wheel? Which one is more clear? Which one sounds more interesting?* (the second one) *Why is it better?* (e.g., tells more, sounds exciting) Then guide students through the activities.

- **Activity A:** Say: *These writers started with good topics. Can you guess what they are?* Read the first story aloud. Ask: *What do you think was the topic?* If students say "a dog," guide them to understand that this story is about one dog that can do something special. A better topic is "Cha-Cha, the dancing dog."

- **Activity B (Convention):** Say: *The names on this page are missing something. What is it?* (capital letters) Guide students to use proofreading marks to indicate the letters that should be capitalized.

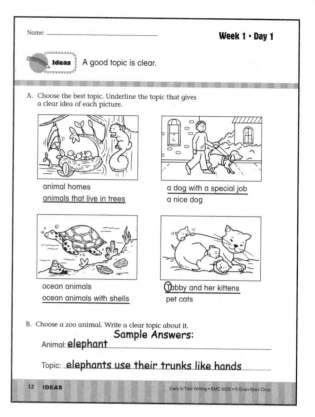

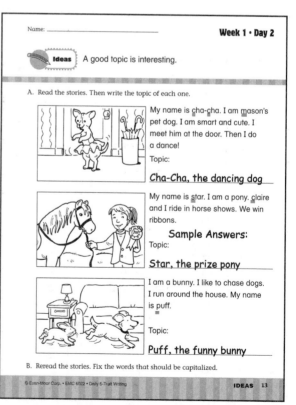

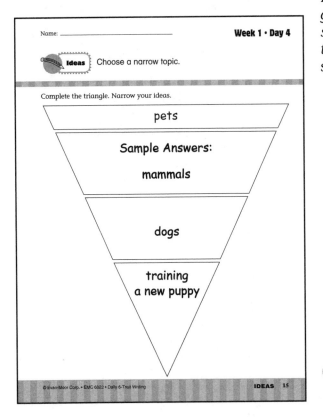

Name: _____   **Week 1 • Day 3**

Ideas Choose a specific topic.

Read each topic. Write two ways to make the topic more interesting. Circle the one you like best.

Topic: fun at school

1. Sample Answer: singing silly
2. songs in music class

Topic: uncommon pets

1. Sample Answer: my friend has
2. to feed her snake live mice

Topic: eating dinner

1. Sample Answer: my dad's
2. famous veggie lasagna

Topic: bears

1. Sample Answer: my mom saw a
2. bear while hiking

14   IDEAS   Daily 6-Trait Writing • EMC 6022 • © Evan-Moor Corp.

Name: _____   **Week 1 • Day 4**

Ideas Choose a narrow topic.

Complete the triangle. Narrow your ideas.

pets

Sample Answers:

mammals

dogs

training
a new puppy

© Evan-Moor Corp. • EMC 6022 • Daily 6-Trait Writing   IDEAS   15

DAY 3

Read the rule aloud. Ask: *Do you remember what makes a good topic?* (It is clear and interesting.) *A good topic should also be specific.* Give examples. (e.g., show and tell; the time Mary's pet rat escaped and ran around the room) Ask: *Which one is more specific?* (the second) Say: *The second one is more specific because it tells what happened during a certain show and tell.* Then guide students through the activity.

• Point out the first topic. Ask: *Is "fun at school" very interesting? What topics are more specific that would tell more about fun at school?* (e.g., class wins Field Day; doing an experiment) List students' suggestions on the board. Have students copy ideas from the board or write their own, circling their favorite.

Convention: Remind students to capitalize the names of people and pets.

DAY 4

Read the rule aloud. Then say: *We've learned that a good topic is clear, interesting, and specific. However, sometimes we start with topics that are too big. One way to get a clear idea is to narrow down a topic.* Then guide students through the activity.

• Model narrowing the topic by reproducing and completing the triangle on the board. Say: *The topic **pets** is too big! There are too many things to write about. However, I can narrow it down to "pets I had when I was young." Then I can narrow it down more to "my dog, Fido," and again to "Fido won the pet talent contest."* Point out that you capitalized **Fido.**

• As students complete the activity, circulate to check their topics. For students who have never had a pet, point out that their topic could be about a friend's pet or a pet they would like to have. You may wish to have students work in pairs to help each other brainstorm ideas.

DAY 5 *Writing Prompt*

• *Write about a pet. Use the topic you chose on Day 4.*

• *Be sure to capitalize the names of people and pets.*

Name: _____

Ideas   A good topic is clear.

A. Choose the best topic. Underline the topic that gives a clear idea of each picture.

animal homes
animals that live in trees

a dog with a special job
a nice dog

ocean animals
ocean animals with shells

Tabby and her kittens
pet cats

B. Choose a zoo animal. Write a clear topic about it.

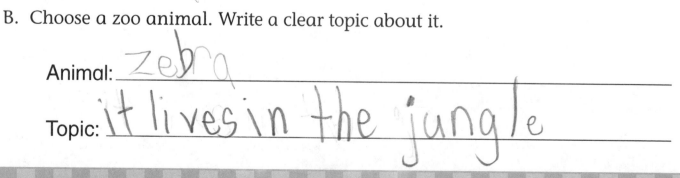

Animal: *zebra*

Topic: *it lives in the jungle*

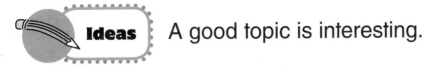

Ideas   A good topic is interesting.

A. Read the stories. Then write the topic of each one.

My name is cha-cha. I am mason's pet dog. I am smart and cute. I meet him at the door. Then I do a dance!

Topic:

Mason's dog Cha-Cha.

My name is star. I am a pony. claire and I ride in horse shows. We win ribbons.

Topic:

Star rides in horse

I am a bunny. I like to chase dogs. I run around the house. My name is puff.

Topic:

Puff chases dogs around the house.

B. Reread the stories. Fix the words that should be capitalized.

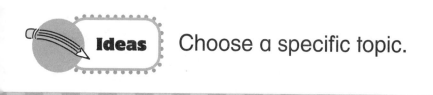 **Ideas** Choose a specific topic.

Read each topic. Write two ways to make the topic more interesting. Circle the one you like best.

Topic: fun at school

1. _____

2. _____

Topic: uncommon pets

1. _____

2. _____

Topic: eating dinner

1. _____

2. _____

Topic: bears

1. _____

2. _____

Ideas   Choose a narrow topic.

Complete the triangle. Narrow your ideas.

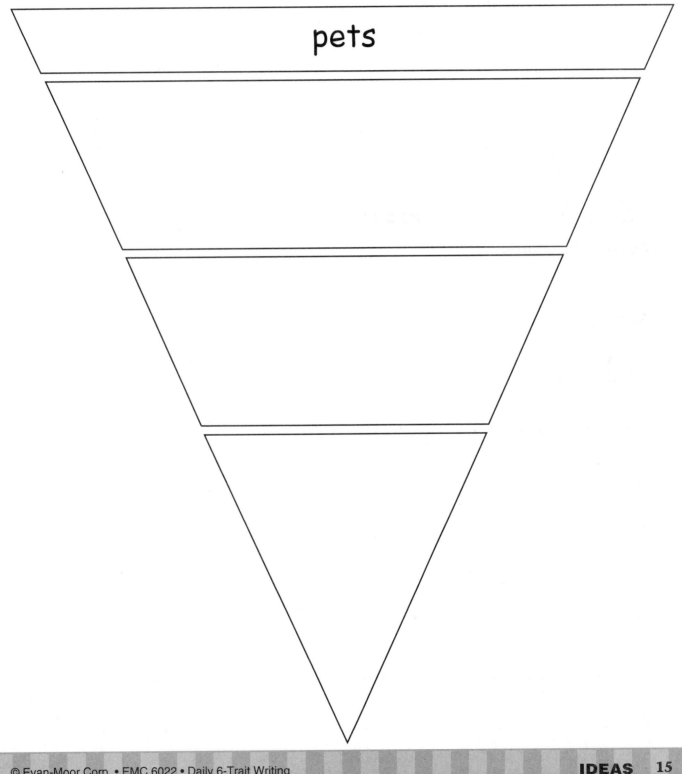

pets

DAY 1

Read the rule aloud and introduce the concept of details. Display an item of clothing such as a sweater or sweatshirt. Say: *Let's pretend this sweater is our "topic." What are some things you could tell about it?* List students' suggestions on the board. (e.g., color, size, fabric, buttons) Then write the word **details** above the list and say: *All of these things are* **details**. *They tell more about the sweater.* Then guide students through the activities.

- **Activity A:** Inquire if students have ever sent or received a thank-you note. Ask: *What details are good to put in a thank-you note?* (reasons why you like something, what made it special, etc.) Have a student read aloud Carlos's note. Ask: *What is the topic of the note?* (new raincoat) *What are some details Carlos gives about why he liked it?* (matches brown boots, has a hood, etc.) Have students underline the details.

  Convention: Introduce or review the definition of a compound word. (a word made from two smaller words) Give examples such as **sweatshirt**, **necktie**, and **outdoors**. Then have students complete the activity.

- **Activity B:** Say: *The details Carlos gives help us "see" the raincoat in our minds. Use those details to draw what you see.* If necessary, model how to label a picture.

DAY 2

Read the rule aloud to review the concept of details. Then ask: *Have you ever read a story about someone's life?* Inform students that today they will be reading a story that is not about a person's life, but about the life of a shoe! Then ask: *Can you predict what kinds of details we might read about the life of a shoe?* (e.g., how it was made, whom it belongs to, who wears it, where it goes, where it sleeps, what it looks like) Then guide students through the activities.

- **Activity A:** Have students read the story "A Shoe Is Born" and work in pairs to identify the details.

- **Activity B (Convention):** Review compound words. Have students find and write the four compound words from the story.

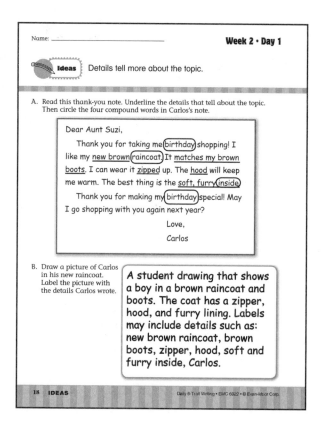

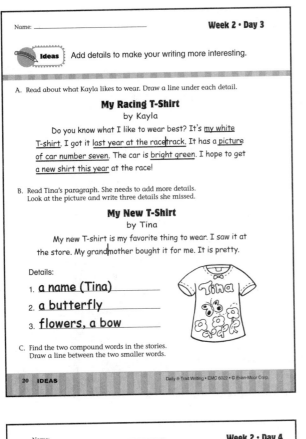

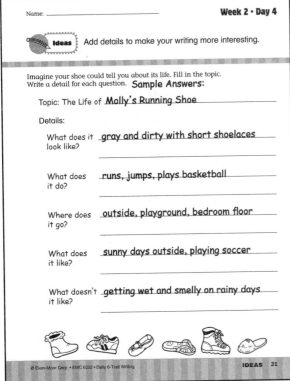

Read the rule aloud. Write the following sentences on the board: *1) The lady had a big hat. 2) The tiny lady's huge purple hat was the first thing I noticed.* Ask: *Which sentence is more interesting?* (sentence 2) *Why?* (It has more details. It tells more things about the lady and her hat.) Have students identify the details in sentence 2. Then guide students through the activities.

- **Activity A:** Have students work in pairs to complete the activity. Then have them share what they underlined.

- **Activity B:** Help students recognize the missing details by asking questions, such as: *What is on the T-shirt? Why does Tina think it is pretty?*

- **Activity C (Convention):** Review compound words. On the board, model how to draw a line between the smaller words. (e.g., rain|bow)

Say: *Look at your shoe. Imagine what its life might be like.* To elicit ideas and details from students, ask: *What does it look like? Is it old or young? Does it have a hard life or an easy one? Where does it go in a day? What does it like to do? What doesn't it like?* Then guide students through the activity.

Refer students to the organizer. Prompt students to choose a good topic by thinking of specific shoes to complete the topic frame. (e.g., The Life of Molly's Running Shoe, The Life of Marco's Sandal) Then have them write a detail about their shoe's life to answer each question. If necessary, model completing the organizer on the board. Encourage students to use at least one compound word.

Writing Prompt

- *Imagine your shoe could tell you about its life. Write what it would say. Use the details you listed on Day 4 to make your writing more interesting.*

- *Try to use at least one compound word in your writing.*

 **Ideas** ⋮ Details tell more about the topic.

A. Read this thank-you note. Underline the details that tell about the topic. Then circle the four compound words in Carlos's note.

> Dear Aunt Suzi,
>
> Thank you for taking me birthday shopping! I like my new brown raincoat. It matches my brown boots. I can wear it zipped up. The hood will keep me warm. The best thing is the soft, furry inside.
>
> Thank you for making my birthday special! May I go shopping with you again next year?
>
> Love,
>
> Carlos

B. Draw a picture of Carlos in his new raincoat. Label the picture with the details Carlos wrote.

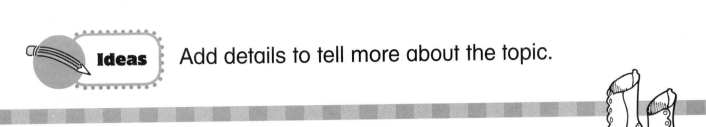

Ideas   Add details to tell more about the topic.

A. Read this story. Then list four details you read.

A Shoe Is Born

I was born in a poor old shoemaker's shop. He cut me out of his very last piece of leather. Then he placed me on his workbench. He went home. Late that night, two tiny elves danced into the shop. The elves worked and worked until sunrise. Then they ran off. The next morning, the shoemaker had a big surprise. I was a pair of beautiful red shoes!

1. _____

2. _____

3. _____

4. _____

B. Write the four different compound words in the story.

_____   _____

_____   _____

Ideas Add details to make your writing more interesting.

A. Read about what Kayla likes to wear. Draw a line under each detail.

My Racing T-Shirt
by Kayla

Do you know what I like to wear best? It's my white T-shirt. I got it last year at the racetrack. It has a picture of car number seven. The car is bright green. I hope to get a new shirt this year at the race!

B. Read Tina's paragraph. She needs to add more details. Look at the picture and write three details she missed.

My New T-Shirt
by Tina

My new T-shirt is my favorite thing to wear. I saw it at the store. My grandmother bought it for me. It is pretty.

Details:

1. _____

2. _____

3. _____

C. Find the two compound words in the stories. Draw a line between the two smaller words.

Ideas | Add details to make your writing more interesting.

Imagine your shoe could tell you about its life. Fill in the topic.
Write a detail for each question.

Topic: The Life of _____

Details:

What does it
look like? _____

_____

What does
it do? _____

_____

Where does
it go? _____

_____

What does
it like? _____

_____

What doesn't
it like? _____

_____

IDEAS
Choose Better Details

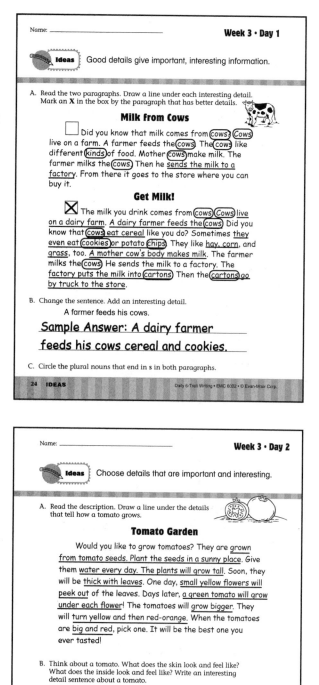

DAY 1

Read the rule aloud. Then say: *Some details are more important or more interesting than others.* Ask: *Which is more interesting: A) Cows eat a lot, or B) Cows eat cereal, cookies, and potato chips left over from factories?* (B) *Why?* (It gives more information. It's interesting to know that cows eat some things people eat.) Then guide students through the activities.

- **Activity A:** Read the two paragraphs aloud. Have students underline the details they think are most interesting. Then ask questions to help students compare the details in both. For example: *Which paragraph tells more about where cows live?* (Paragraph 2: a dairy farm vs. a farm) *Which one tells how milk gets to the store?* (Paragraph 2: by truck in cartons) Have students mark the paragraph that has better details.

- **Activity B:** Ask students to name details they just read about what cows eat. Then have them use those details to change the sentence into one that is more interesting. (e.g., A dairy farmer feeds his cows cookies.)

- **Activity C (Convention):** Remind students that a plural noun names more than one person, place, or thing. Help them locate the plural nouns in the paragraphs and circle them.

DAY 2

Read the rule aloud. Then say: *Details are very important in a description. Details help you "see" what you're reading about.* Then guide students through the activities.

- **Activity A:** Read the description together and discuss which details tell how a tomato grows. Have students draw a line under each detail.

- **Activity B:** Ask students to describe the inside and outside of a tomato. List key words and phrases on the board. (e.g., smooth, shiny, soft, squishy, juicy, full of seeds) Then have students complete the activity and read aloud their new detail sentences.

- **Activity C (Convention):** Model how to add an s to the end of a noun to make it plural.

Name: _____   Week 3 • Day 3

Ideas   Choose details that are important and interesting.

A. Read the paragraph. Then write a sentence with an interesting detail to add to the end of the story.

From the Field to Your Lunch

Do you have a slice of bread in your lunch today? It came from a farmer's field! Here's how it happened. A farmer plowed up his field. Next, he planted wheat seeds. He watered the wheat. He got rid of bugs and weeds. When the wheat was ripe, the farmer picked it. If bad weather came, it could hurt the wheat. So he worked for days to pick it. Then, he sold the wheat. It was ground into flour, and the flour was baked into bread.

Ending Sentence:

Sample Answer: The bread was
used to make a turkey sandwich
for your lunch.

B. Write four nouns from the story that name more than one person, place, or thing.

seeds   bugs
weeds   days

26   IDEAS   Daily 6-Trait Writing • EMC 6022 • © Evan-Moor Corp.

Name: _____   Week 3 • Day 4

Ideas   Choose details that are important and interesting.

Tell about your favorite bread. Write interesting details.

Topic:
My favorite bread: **Sample Answers:**
                      tortilla

Details:
What I eat on it: cheese and meat

When I eat it: dinner

Where I eat it: at home

Whom I eat it with: my family

Why I like it: it is soft and tastes good

How I like to eat it: as an enchilada

© Evan-Moor Corp. • EMC 6022 • Daily 6-Trait Writing   IDEAS   27

DAY 3

Read the rule aloud. Then say: *In this paragraph, you will read interesting details about a food that most people eat every day.* Then guide students through the activities.

- **Activity A:** Have students read the paragraph and name some interesting details they found in it. Then have students suggest ideas of sentences to add to the end of the story. Ask: *What kind of bread could have been baked? What happened to the bread?* (e.g., The bread was used to make a sandwich for your lunch.)

- **Activity B (Convention):** Remind students that a plural noun names more than one person, place, or thing and ends in **s**. If necessary, work as a class to find the plural nouns.

DAY 4

Read the rule aloud. Then guide students to complete the activity.

- Say: *Today, we are going to plan a paragraph about our favorite bread. First, we need to think of important and interesting details.* Guide students in choosing their favorite kind of bread and completing the 5 **Ws** and **H** chart.

- Help students brainstorm by asking prompting questions, such as: *What kinds of bread do you eat?* (e.g., whole wheat, tortillas, corn bread, rolls, biscuits, bagels) *What do you eat on it?* (e.g., butter, cheese) *When do you eat it?* (e.g., breakfast, after school) *Where do you eat it?* (e.g., picnic, restaurant) *Whom do you eat bread with?* (e.g., my grandma after she bakes it) *Why do you like it?* (e.g., soft, homemade) *How do you like to eat bread?* (e.g., toasted, as a sandwich, in soup) Have students share their ideas.

DAY 5   *Writing Prompt*

- *Describe a kind of bread you like. Use the important and interesting details you listed on Day 4.*

- *Look at what you wrote. Did you use any plural nouns that end in s? Draw a line under each one.*

Ideas : Good details give important, interesting information.

A. Read the two paragraphs. Draw a line under each interesting detail. Mark an **X** in the box by the paragraph that has better details.

Milk from Cows

☐ Did you know that milk comes from cows? Cows live on a farm. A farmer feeds the cows. The cows like different kinds of food. Mother cows make milk. The farmer milks the cows. Then he sends the milk to a factory. From there it goes to the store where you can buy it.

Get Milk!

☐ The milk you drink comes from cows. Cows live on a dairy farm. A dairy farmer feeds the cows. Did you know that cows eat cereal like you do? Sometimes they even eat cookies or potato chips. They like hay, corn, and grass, too. A mother cow's body makes milk. The farmer milks the cows. He sends the milk to a factory. The factory puts the milk into cartons. Then the cartons go by truck to the store.

B. Change the sentence. Add an interesting detail.

   A farmer feeds his cows.

   _____

   _____

C. Circle the plural nouns that end in **s** in both paragraphs.

Daily 6-Trait Writing • EMC 6022 • © Evan-Moor Corp.

 **Ideas**   Choose details that are important and interesting.

A. Read the description. Draw a line under the details that tell how a tomato grows.

Tomato Garden

Would you like to grow tomatoes? They are grown from tomato seeds. Plant the seeds in a sunny place. Give them water every day. The plants will grow tall. Soon, they will be thick with leaves. One day, small yellow flowers will peek out of the leaves. Days later, a green tomato will grow under each flower! The tomatoes will grow bigger. They will turn yellow and then red-orange. When the tomatoes are big and red, pick one. It will be the best one you ever tasted!

B. Think about a tomato. What does the skin look and feel like? What does the inside look and feel like? Write an interesting detail sentence about a tomato.

_____

_____

C. Make these nouns plural. Add an **s**.

seed____   plant____   flower____   day____

 **Ideas** Choose details that are important and interesting.

A. Read the paragraph. Then write a sentence with an interesting detail to add to the end of the story.

From the Field to Your Lunch

Do you have a slice of bread in your lunch today? It came from a farmer's field! Here's how it happened. A farmer plowed up his field. Next, he planted wheat seeds. He watered the wheat. He got rid of bugs and weeds. When the wheat was ripe, the farmer picked it. If bad weather came, it could hurt the wheat. So he worked for days to pick it. Then, he sold the wheat. It was ground into flour, and the flour was baked into bread.

Ending Sentence:

_____

_____

_____

B. Write four nouns from the story that name more than one person, place, or thing.

_____   _____

_____   _____

 **Ideas** Choose details that are important and interesting.

Tell about your favorite bread. Write interesting details.

Topic:

My favorite bread: _____

Details:

What I eat on it: _____

When I eat it: _____

Where I eat it: _____

Whom I eat it with: _____

Why I like it: _____

How I like to eat it: _____

DAY 1

Read the rule aloud. Say: *When we write, we need to be sure all our details stick to the topic. If we don't stick to the topic and write about too many things, our reader may become confused.* Read this paragraph and ask students to listen for a detail that doesn't stick to the topic: *Mercedes brought her lunch to school today. She brought an apple, crackers, and peanut butter. Last night, her baby sister had the hiccups. Mercedes packed a juice box, too.* Ask: *Which detail <u>didn't</u> belong?* (her baby sister having the hiccups) Then guide students through the activities.

• **Activity A:** Have a student describe the first picture. Ask: *Does this picture stick to the topic of liking Blue Sky Elementary?* (yes) *Why?* (It's about eating lunch with friends at school.) Repeat for the remaining pictures.

• **Activity B:** Ask: *Based on the pictures, why does the writer like Blue Sky Elementary?* (eating lunch with friends; using computer lab) Have students write phrases describing the pictures.

Convention: To review the convention of end punctuation, take one of the phrases a student wrote in Activity B and turn it into a sentence. (e.g., It is fun to eat lunch with friends in the lunchroom.) Write it on the board. Then ask: *What kind of sentence is this?* (telling) *What end punctuation does a telling sentence have?* (a period) Circle the period in the sentence.

DAY 2

Review the rule. Then say: *Remember that when you write, it is important to include only details that stick to the topic. If a writer doesn't stick to the topic, the reader may become confused.* Then guide students through the activities.

• **Activity A:** Read story 1 aloud. Ask: *What is the topic of these sentences?* (a quiz about a book) *Which sentence <u>doesn't</u> stick to the topic?* ("Megan is my friend.") Have students complete the activity on their own or in pairs.

• **Activity B:** To help students generate ideas, ask: *What details could we add to story 3's topic?* (e.g., woke up late; caught the bus just in time) Then say: *Write a telling sentence to add to story 3. Be sure to use a period at the end.* Have students share their sentences.

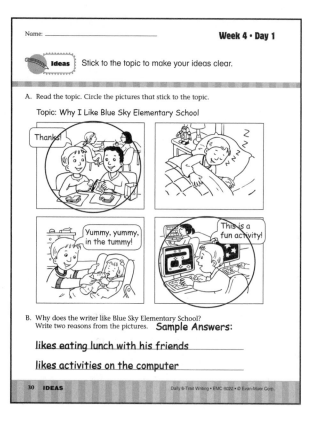

Name: _____   **Week 4 • Day 1**

Ideas Stick to the topic to make your ideas clear.

A. Read the topic. Circle the pictures that stick to the topic.

Topic: Why I Like Blue Sky Elementary School

B. Why does the writer like Blue Sky Elementary School? Write two reasons from the pictures. **Sample Answers:**

likes eating lunch with his friends _____

likes activities on the computer _____

30 IDEAS   Daily 6-Trait Writing • EMC 6022 • © Evan-Moor Corp.

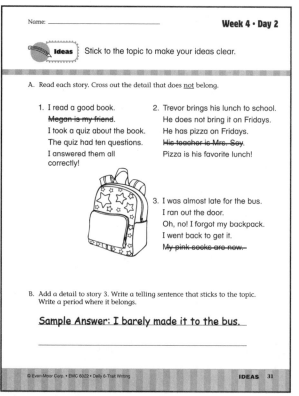

Name: _____   **Week 4 • Day 2**

Ideas Stick to the topic to make your ideas clear.

A. Read each story. Cross out the detail that does <u>not</u> belong.

1. I read a good book.
~~Megan is my friend.~~
I took a quiz about the book.
The quiz had ten questions.
I answered them all correctly!

2. Trevor brings his lunch to school.
He does not bring it on Fridays.
He has pizza on Fridays.
~~His teacher is Mrs. Say.~~
Pizza is his favorite lunch!

3. I was almost late for the bus.
I ran out the door.
Oh, no! I forgot my backpack.
I went back to get it.
~~My pink socks are new.~~

B. Add a detail to story 3. Write a telling sentence that sticks to the topic. Write a period where it belongs.

Sample Answer: I barely made it to the bus.

_____

© Evan-Moor Corp. • EMC 6022 • Daily 6-Trait Writing   **IDEAS** 31

Worksheet: Week 4 · Day 3

Name: _____   **Week 4 · Day 3**

Ideas Stick to the topic to make your ideas clear.

A. Read the story. Cross out the two sentences that do <u>not</u> stick to the topic.

New at School

My teacher says we will have a new student. Her name is Kamry. We talked about how to help her. We can show her where to put her coat. We can sit by her in the lunchroom. She can play with us on the playground. ~~I like to sing in music class.~~ We can show her where to line up. She can sit with me on the bus. ~~I like math best.~~

B. Write two new sentences to add to the story. Make sure that they stick to the topic. Put periods where they belong.

1. **Sample Answers:**

   We can tell her how to buy lunch.

2. **We can show her the restroom.**

Worksheet: Week 4 · Day 4

Name: _____   **Week 4 · Day 4**

Ideas Stick to the topic to make your ideas clear.

Add up the details. Think of things that make your school special. Write them in the boxes.

Detail: **Sample Answers:**
         nice teachers

+

Detail: **fun art classes**

+

Detail: **big computer lab**

+

Detail: **many field trips**

=

Topic: **My School Is Special**

DAY 3

Review the rule. Set the stage for the activity by asking: *What could we do to help a new student feel welcome in our class?* (e.g., show how to buy lunch; point out the restroom; invite to sit with us) Write students' ideas on the board. Then guide students through the activities.

- **Activity A:** Have students complete the activity independently and then share which sentences they crossed out and why.

- **Activity B:** To help students think of sentences, invite them to refer to the list of ideas on the board and use any that are not already in the paragraph. Remind students to place a period at the end of telling sentences. Then invite students to share their sentences.

DAY 4

Review the rule. Then say: *Tomorrow's writing activity is about our school. Can you name some details that make our school special?* Encourage students to contribute ideas as you write them on the board. (e.g., class plays; art and music classes; uniforms)

- Then guide students to complete the graphic organizer for Day 4, using the ideas brainstormed by the class. Point out that the boxes on this page are stacked like a math problem. Direct students to write a detail in each box. Say: *Make sure all your details "add up" to the topic "My School Is Special."* Model completing the organizer on the board. (e.g., nice teachers, fun art classes, big computer lab, many field trips)

- Then have students exchange their papers with a neighbor. Direct them to check their neighbor's paper for details that stick to the topic.

DAY 5 *Writing Prompt*

- *Write about what makes your school special. Begin with the topic. Then give details that stick to the topic. Use your ideas from the graphic organizer on Day 4.*

- *Be sure to write a period at the end of each telling sentence.*

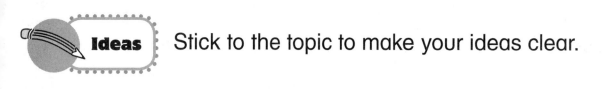

Ideas   Stick to the topic to make your ideas clear.

A. Read the topic. Circle the pictures that stick to the topic.

Topic: Why I Like Blue Sky Elementary School

B. Why does the writer like Blue Sky Elementary School?
   Write two reasons from the pictures.

_____

_____

 **Ideas** Stick to the topic to make your ideas clear.

A. Read each story. Cross out the detail that does <u>not</u> belong.

1. I read a good book.
   Megan is my friend.
   I took a quiz about the book.
   The quiz had ten questions.
   I answered them all correctly!

2. Trevor brings his lunch to school.
   He does not bring it on Fridays.
   He has pizza on Fridays.
   His teacher is Mrs. Sey.
   Pizza is his favorite lunch!

3. I was almost late for the bus.
   I ran out the door.
   Oh, no! I forgot my backpack.
   I went back to get it.
   My pink socks are new.

B. Add a detail to story 3. Write a telling sentence that sticks to the topic.
   Write a period where it belongs.

_____

_____

Ideas   Stick to the topic to make your ideas clear.

A. Read the story. Cross out the two sentences that do <u>not</u> stick to the topic.

New at School

    My teacher says we will have a new student. Her
name is Kamry. We talked about how to help her. We can
show her where to put her coat. We can sit by her in the
lunchroom. She can play with us on the playground. I like
to sing in music class. We can show her where to line up.
She can sit with me on the bus. I like math best.

B. Write two new sentences to add to the story. Make sure that they stick
to the topic. Put periods where they belong.

1. _____

    _____

2. _____

    _____

     Daily 6-Trait Writing • EMC 6022 • © Evan-Moor Corp.

 **Ideas** Stick to the topic to make your ideas clear.

Add up the details. Think of things that make your school special.
Write them in the boxes.

Detail:

_____

+

Detail:

_____

+

Detail:

_____

+

Detail:

_____

=

Topic:

_____

DAY 1

Review the rule. Remind students that a good topic is a clear idea that is interesting and specific. Then guide students through the activities.

- **Activity A:** Have students look at the first picture and tell a partner what they see. Then ask: *Which topic better describes the picture?* (Uncle Joe playing the violin) *Why?* (e.g., It tells more details. It gives a clear, specific idea.) Repeat the process for the second picture.

- **Activity B:** Have students look carefully at each picture and imagine what is going on in each scene. (e.g., a school choir giving a special performance; two boys starting a rock band) Encourage students to make up names for the people and places to make the topics as specific as possible. Have students share their topics to check for clarity and precision.

Convention: Help students locate the two song titles on this page. Say: *Important words in a song or book title need capital letters.* Have students identify and circle the important words that are capitalized in the titles.

Name: _____   **Week 5 • Day 1**

 Ideas   Choose a good topic that makes your ideas clear.

A. Draw a line under the best topic for each picture.

the nice music
Uncle Joe playing the violin
America the Beautiful

singing "Home" on the Range
playing music
life on a ranch

B. Write a good topic for each picture. Make your ideas clear.

Sample Answers:

the school choir
singing "Puff, the
Magic Dragon"

my brother and his best
friend pretending to be
rock stars

36 IDEAS   Daily 6-Trait Writing • EMC 6022 • © Evan-Moor Corp.

DAY 2

Review the rule. To demonstrate the rule, describe a game in two ways. First, simply name the game you've played. Then give a complete description. Ask: *Which description tells more about the game?* (the second) Say: *Details give readers more information about the topic. Often, those details help us picture the topic in our minds.* Then guide students through the activities.

- **Activity A:** Have students close their eyes as you read aloud the report. Explain that they should picture the scene in their minds as you read.

- **Activity B:** Ask: *What pictures did the writer help you see?* (e.g., Grandpa carefully shining his shoes) *Which details does the author think are important?* (e.g., what Grandpa takes out of the trunk; how the children feel)

- **Activity C (Convention):** Have students find and circle the capital letters in the book titles. Point out that only important words are capitalized. Words such as **and, the,** and **of** are not.

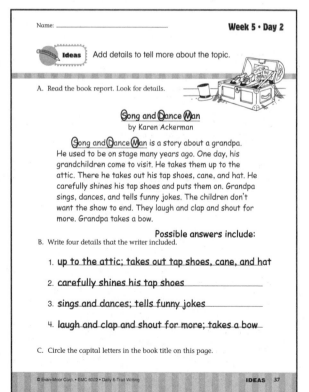

Name: _____   **Week 5 • Day 2**

Ideas   Add details to tell more about the topic.

A. Read the book report. Look for details.

Song and Dance Man
by Karen Ackerman

Song and Dance Man is a story about a grandpa. He used to be on stage many years ago. One day, his grandchildren come to visit. He takes them up to the attic. There he takes out his tap shoes, cane, and hat. He carefully shines his tap shoes and puts them on. Grandpa sings, dances, and tells funny jokes. The children don't want the show to end. They laugh and clap and shout for more. Grandpa takes a bow.

Possible answers include:

B. Write four details that the writer included.

1. up to the attic; takes out tap shoes, cane, and hat

2. carefully shines his tap shoes

3. sings and dances; tells funny jokes

4. laugh and clap and shout for more; takes a bow

C. Circle the capital letters in the book title on this page.

© Evan-Moor Corp. • EMC 6022 • Daily 6-Trait Writing   **IDEAS** 37

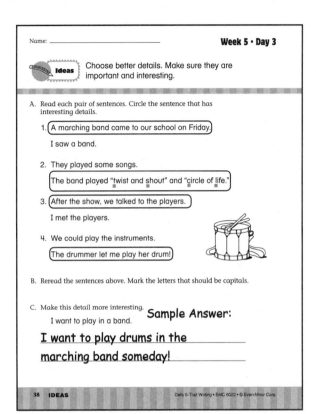

Name: _____ **Week 5 • Day 3**

Ideas Choose better details. Make sure they are important and interesting.

A. Read each pair of sentences. Circle the sentence that has interesting details.

1. A marching band came to our school on Friday.

   I saw a band.

2. They played some songs.

   The band played "twist and shout" and "circle of life."

3. After the show, we talked to the players.

   I met the players.

4. We could play the instruments.

   The drummer let me play her drum!

B. Reread the sentences above. Mark the letters that should be capitals.

C. Make this detail more interesting. **Sample Answer:**

   I want to play in a band.

   I want to play drums in the marching band someday!

38 IDEAS   Daily 6-Trait Writing • EMC 6022 • © Evan-Moor Corp.

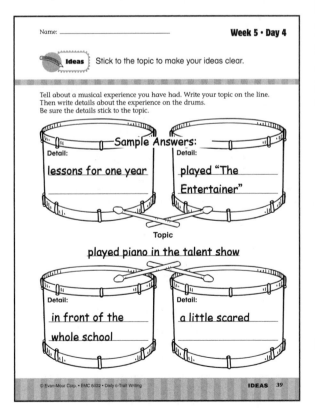

Name: _____ **Week 5 • Day 4**

Ideas Stick to the topic to make your ideas clear.

Tell about a musical experience you have had. Write your topic on the line.
Then write details about the experience on the drums.
Be sure the details stick to the topic.

Sample Answers:

Detail: lessons for one year

Detail: played "The Entertainer"

Topic

played piano in the talent show

Detail: in front of the whole school

Detail: a little scared

© Evan-Moor Corp. • EMC 6022 • Daily 6-Trait Writing   IDEAS 39

DAY 3

Read the rule aloud. Then write these sentences on the board: *I used to be in a band. In high school, I played trumpet in the marching band.* Then say: *These two sentences are about the same thing, but the second one is better. Why?* (it is more interesting; gives important details) Then guide students through the activities.

- **Activity A:** Have students work with a partner to read each pair of sentences and discuss which one is better.

- **Activity B (Convention):** Have students use proofreading marks to identify the words that need capital letters. Ask students why those letters should be capitalized. (song titles)

- **Activity C:** Read the sentence. Then say: *Now that you've seen examples of more interesting sentences, you can write one of your own. What details could we add to this sentence?* Write students' ideas on the board. Then have students write their own sentences and read them aloud.

DAY 4

Read the rule aloud. Invite students to share a musical memory. Ask questions to jog their memories, such as: *Have you seen a band or choir? Do you know someone who plays music? Does a certain song remind you of anything or anyone?* Then guide students through the activities.

- If necessary, provide a sentence starter for the topic. (e.g., "My favorite musical memory is...") After students fill in their topics, have them write details on the drums. Point out that each drum connects to the topic to remind students that details must stick to the topic.

- Have students exchange papers with a partner to improve their details. Ask questions such as: *Do your partner's details stick to the topic? How can your partner's details be more interesting? Give suggestions to your partner to improve his or her details.*

DAY 5 *Writing Prompt*

- *Write a journal entry telling about a musical experience you have had. Use the topic and interesting details you thought of on Day 4.*

- *Be sure to capitalize the titles of books and songs.*

 **Ideas**) Choose a good topic that makes your ideas clear.

A. Draw a line under the best topic for each picture.

the nice music

Uncle Joe playing the violin

"America the Beautiful"

singing "Home on the Range"

playing music

life on a ranch

B. Write a good topic for each picture. Make your ideas clear.

_____   _____

_____   _____

_____   _____

 **Ideas** Add details to tell more about the topic.

A. Read the book report. Look for details.

Song and Dance Man
by Karen Ackerman

Song and Dance Man is a story about a grandpa. He used to be on stage many years ago. One day, his grandchildren come to visit. He takes them up to the attic. There he takes out his tap shoes, cane, and hat. He carefully shines his tap shoes and puts them on. Grandpa sings, dances, and tells funny jokes. The children don't want the show to end. They laugh and clap and shout for more. Grandpa takes a bow.

B. Write four details that the writer included.

1. _____

2. _____

3. _____

4. _____

C. Circle the capital letters in the book title on this page.

Ideas

Choose better details. Make sure they are important and interesting.

A. Read each pair of sentences. Circle the sentence that has interesting details.

1. A marching band came to our school on Friday.

   I saw a band.

2. They played some songs.

   The band played "twist and shout" and "circle of life."

3. After the show, we talked to the players.

   I met the players.

4. We could play the instruments.

   The drummer let me play her drum!

B. Reread the sentences above. Mark the letters that should be capitals.

C. Make this detail more interesting.

   I want to play in a band.

   _____

   _____

Daily 6-Trait Writing • EMC 6022 • © Evan-Moor Corp.

 **Ideas** Stick to the topic to make your ideas clear.

Tell about a musical experience you have had. Write your topic on the line.
Then write details about the experience on the drums.
Be sure the details stick to the topic.

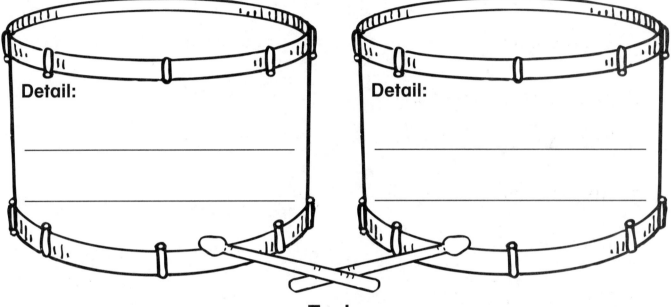

Detail:

_____

_____

Detail:

_____

_____

Topic

_____

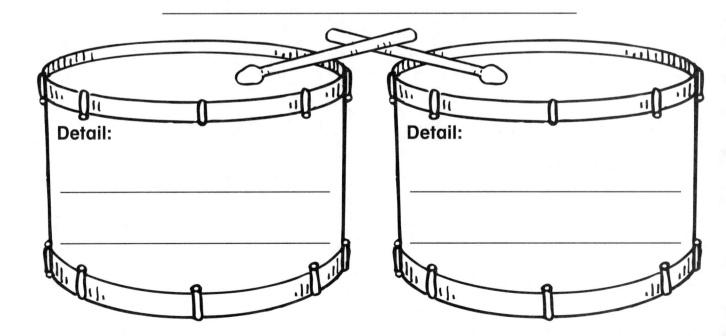

Detail:

_____

_____

Detail:

_____

_____

ORGANIZATION
Put Things in the Right Order

Refer to pages 6 and 7 to introduce or review the writing trait.

DAY 1

Invite students to imagine themselves washing their hands and to think about the steps involved. (turn on faucet, pump soap, make lather, rinse, turn off faucet, dry) Then ask: *What would happen if the steps were <u>not</u> done in the right order?* (Hands wouldn't get clean.) Explain: *When we write, it is important to put things in the right order. This helps the reader understand our ideas. Putting things in order is one kind of organization.* Write the word **organization** on the board. Then guide students through the activities.

- **Activity A:** Read aloud the paragraph, emphasizing **first, next, then,** and **last.** Say: *The words **first, next, then,** and **last** are order words. They help us identify the order in which things happen.* Have students find and circle those words in the paragraph.

- **Activity B:** Ask: *What do you do first to gather seeds? Draw it in the box. What do you do next?* Continue with the remaining boxes.

Convention: Say: *A sentence is a group of words that makes up a complete thought.* Write on the board: *Seeds will stick to the sock.* Say: *This is a sentence because it is a complete thought. It tells us what the seeds will do.* Then write the fragments "stick to" and "Seeds will." Ask: *Are these complete thoughts? Are they sentences?* (no)

DAY 2

Read the rule aloud and review the concept of order. Then guide students through the activity.

- Say: *By using order, you can describe how something happens.* First, ask: *Where does a tree get its food?* (e.g., sun, water, and soil) Then say: *Trees get and make their food in a certain order.*

- Have students read the labels and identify where things are on the tree diagram. Then ask: *What part of the tree would you start with to describe the process of how it makes food?* (at the bottom) *Why?* (that's where the tree first gets water and minerals)

Convention: Remind students to write complete sentences. Have them trade papers with a partner to check for complete sentences.

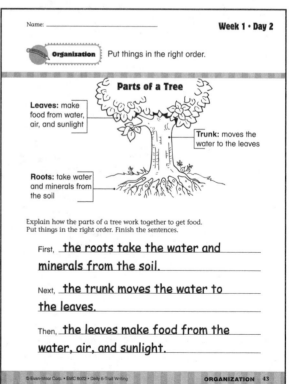

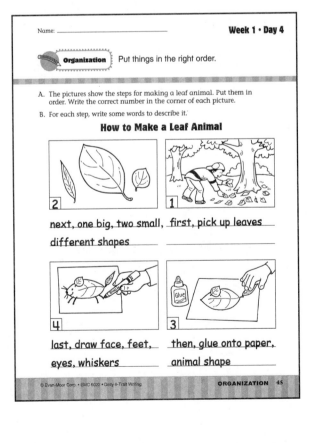

Name: _____ Week 1 • Day 3

Organization Put things in the right order.

Read these sentences. Use them to complete the paragraph below.

Sentences

Then, put birdseed on a paper plate.
Next, spread peanut butter on the pine cone.
Now it's ready to hang in a tree.
First, tie a ribbon around the top of the pine cone.

Pine Cone Bird Feeder

Make a bird feeder for your bird friends. You will need

ribbon, a spoon, a paper plate, a pine cone, peanut butter, and

some birdseed. **First, tie a ribbon around the top of the pine cone.** Leave a long piece of ribbon

for hanging. **Next, spread peanut butter on the pine cone.** Fill in all the spaces. **Then, put birdseed on a paper plate.** Roll the sticky pine

cone in the birdseed. Cover it with birdseed. **Now it's ready to hang in a tree.** Watch to see who comes

to eat!

44 ORGANIZATION   Daily 6-Trait Writing • EMC 6022 • © Evan-Moor Corp.

DAY 3

Review the rule. To review the concept of order, have students think about something they know how to make, such as a paper airplane. Then have them explain the process. Encourage them to use order words. Say: *You used order, a kind of organization, to tell how you made something.* Then guide students through the activity.

- Read the sentences and paragraph aloud. Say: *This paragraph is missing some sentences that tell **how**. We need to add the sentences in the right order.*

- Read the paragraph again, stopping at the first blank. Ask: *Which sentence should go here?* ("First, tie a ribbon...") *How do you know?* (e.g., the order word **first**; it makes sense) Allow time for students to write the sentence. Repeat for the remaining blanks.

- When the paragraph is complete, have a student read it aloud. Ask: *Are the sentences in the right order? Is this paragraph organized so it makes sense?*

DAY 4

Review the rule. Guide students through the activities.

- **Activity A:** Explain that the pictures show the steps for making a leaf animal, but they are not in the right order. Ask: *What is the correct order for these pictures? How can we find the order?* Have students tell you the correct order and number the pictures accordingly in the small boxes.

- **Activity B:** Say: *Tomorrow, we will write about how to make a leaf animal. First, let's write some words we should include for each step.* Have students write key words or sentence fragments under the pictures of each step. You may wish to have students work with a partner.

DAY 5 *Writing Prompt*

- *Write complete sentences telling how to make a "leaf animal." Use your ideas from Day 4. Begin your sentences with the words **First**, **Next**, **Then**, and **Last**.*

- *Have a partner read your writing to check for complete sentences.*

Name: ____________________

Week 1 • Day 1

Organization Organization is putting things in the right order.

A. Read the instructions about gathering seeds. Circle the order words.

How to Gather Seeds

Would you like to study seeds? Here's how. First, ask an adult to give you an old sock. Next, put the big sock over your shoe. Then, walk through a place that has weeds. The seeds will stick to the sock. Last, take off the sock and pick off the seeds. Put them into a paper cup. You can study your seeds!

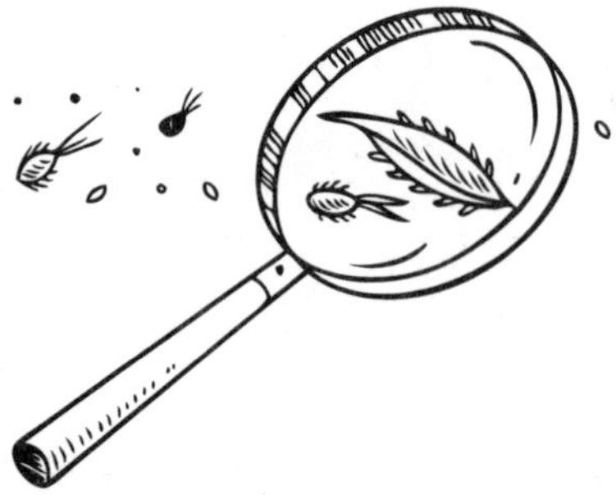

B. Draw four pictures to show how to gather seeds.
Draw things in the right order.

First	Next
Then	Last

Organization Put things in the right order.

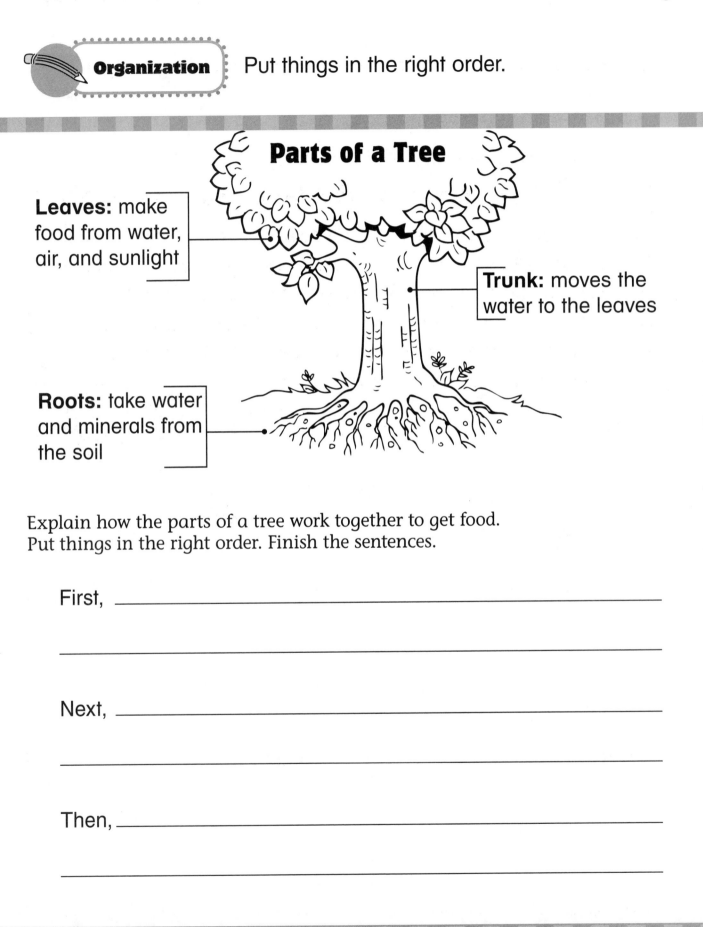

Parts of a Tree

Leaves: make food from water, air, and sunlight

Trunk: moves the water to the leaves

Roots: take water and minerals from the soil

Explain how the parts of a tree work together to get food. Put things in the right order. Finish the sentences.

First, _____

_____

Next, _____

_____

Then, _____

_____

Organization : Put things in the right order.

Read these sentences. Use them to complete the paragraph below.

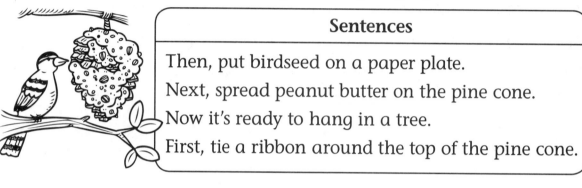

Sentences
Then, put birdseed on a paper plate.
Next, spread peanut butter on the pine cone.
Now it's ready to hang in a tree.
First, tie a ribbon around the top of the pine cone.

Pine Cone Bird Feeder

Make a bird feeder for your bird friends. You will need

ribbon, a spoon, a paper plate, a pine cone, peanut butter, and

some birdseed. _____

_____ Leave a long piece of ribbon

for hanging. _____

_____ Fill in all the spaces. _____

_____ Roll the sticky pine

cone in the birdseed. Cover it with birdseed. _____

_____ Watch to see who comes

to eat!

Organization : Put things in the right order.

A. The pictures show the steps for making a leaf animal. Put them in order. Write the correct number in the corner of each picture.

B. For each step, write some words to describe it.

How to Make a Leaf Animal

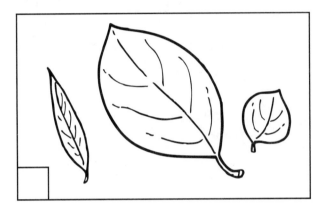

_____

_____

_____

_____

_____

_____

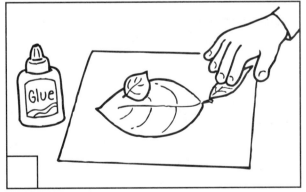

_____

_____

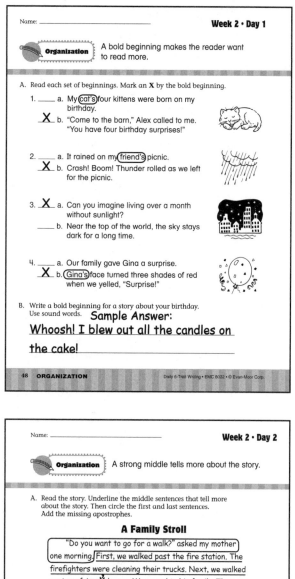

DAY 1

Say: *Each piece of writing should have a beginning, a middle, and an end.* Read the rule aloud. Say: *A beginning introduces what happens in your story. To keep your readers interested, it should be bold!* **Bold** *means "exciting."*

Give these examples: *1) It was Chad's birthday. 2) When Chad came to the table, he discovered a special gold-trimmed dinner plate at his place.* Ask: *Which one is a bold beginning? Which one sounds exciting?* (the second) Then guide students through the activities.

- **Activity A:** For each set of beginnings, ask: *Which beginning makes you want to read more?* Have students mark the bold beginnings. Then talk about what makes the beginnings bold. (use of dialogue, sound words, details, etc.)

- **Activity B:** Ask: *What are some words that represent sounds?* (e.g., **crash, pop**) *Sound words can be bold beginnings because they grab your reader's attention. Use a sound word to write a bold beginning for a story about your birthday.*

Convention: Say: *We add an apostrophe and the letter* **s** *to a noun to show belonging.* Use a student's name and an object to model. Then have students find and circle the three nouns with **'s** in Activity A.

DAY 2

Read the rule aloud. Then guide students through the activities.

- **Activity A:** Have students read the paragraph and underline the middle sentences. Then have students circle the first and last sentences. Say: *The circled sentences are the beginning and the ending. The middle sentences should take the reader from the beginning to the ending by telling more about the story.* Then say: *Two of the words in this paragraph are missing something. What is it?* (apostrophes) Have students fill them in.

- **Activity B:** After reading aloud the beginning and ending, ask: *What details could go in the middle that would take the reader from the beginning to the ending?* Write students' ideas on the board, checking that each one makes sense. After students write their middles, have volunteers read aloud their completed paragraphs.

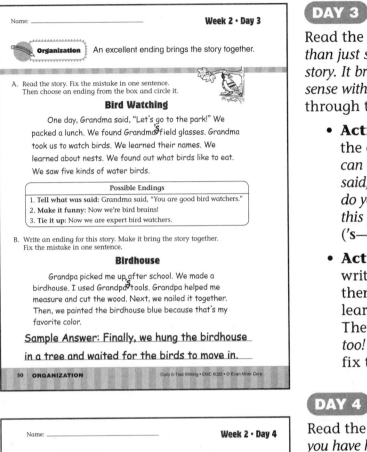

Name: _____   **Week 2 • Day 3**

Organization   An excellent ending brings the story together.

A. Read the story. Fix the mistake in one sentence.
Then choose an ending from the box and circle it.

Bird Watching

One day, Grandma said, "Let's go to the park!" We
packed a lunch. We found Grandma's field glasses. Grandma
took us to watch birds. We learned their names. We
learned about nests. We found out what birds like to eat.
We saw five kinds of water birds.

Possible Endings

1. **Tell what was said:** Grandma said, "You are good bird watchers."
2. **Make it funny:** Now we're bird brains!
3. **Tie it up:** Now we are expert bird watchers.

B. Write an ending for this story. Make it bring the story together.
Fix the mistake in one sentence.

Birdhouse

Grandpa picked me up after school. We made a
birdhouse. I used Grandpa's tools. Grandpa helped me
measure and cut the wood. Next, we nailed it together.
Then, we painted the birdhouse blue because that's my
favorite color.

Sample Answer: Finally, we hung the birdhouse
in a tree and waited for the birds to move in.

50   **ORGANIZATION**   Daily 6-Trait Writing • EMC 6022 • © Evan-Moor Corp.

Name: _____   **Week 2 • Day 4**

Organization   Write a bold beginning, a strong middle,
and an excellent ending.

Tell about a fun time you've had with your family. Draw pictures to show
the beginning, middle, and ending. Then write some important words to
go with your pictures.

Sample Answers:

Beginning

family at table
in restaurant
_____
_____

Middle

sister flings food
at server
_____
_____

Ending

everyone laughs and
leaves the restaurant
_____

© Evan-Moor Corp. • EMC 6022 • Daily 6-Trait Writing   **ORGANIZATION**   51

DAY 3

Read the rule aloud. Then say: *There's more to an ending
than just saying "the end." An excellent ending wraps up the
story. It brings everything in the story together and makes
sense with the beginning and middle.* Guide students
through the activities.

- **Activity A:** Read the story and have students fix
  the error. Then say: *This story needs an ending. We
  can end it in several ways. We can tell what someone
  said, make it funny, or tie up the story. Which ending
  do you want to use? Circle it.* Then say: *A word in
  this paragraph is missing something. What is it?*
  (**'s**—**Grandma's**) Have students fix the error.

- **Activity B:** Have students read the story and
  write their own excellent ending. Encourage
  them to use one of the types of endings they've
  learned. Have volunteers share their endings.
  Then say: *Something is missing in this paragraph,
  too! What is it?* (**'s**—**Grandpa's**) Have students
  fix the error.

DAY 4

Read the rule aloud. Then say: *Think about a fun time
you have had with your family. It could be a trip, an event, or
simply a time when everyone laughed.* Give an example.
(e.g., the time your sister accidentally flung food across
a restaurant) Invite students to share their ideas.

- Then say: *Draw the beginning, middle, and end of
  that fun time.* Quickly model this on the board
  (e.g., beginning: family at table in restaurant;
  middle: sister flings food; end: everyone laughs
  and leaves restaurant)

- Have students write some key words or phrases
  to describe the pictures that will help them write
  a bold beginning, strong middle, and excellent
  ending. Remind them to add **'s** to words that
  show belonging.

DAY 5   *Writing Prompt*

- *Write about a fun time you have had with your
  family. Be sure to write a bold beginning, a strong
  middle, and an excellent ending. Use the pictures
  and words from Day 4 to help you.*

- *Remember to add* **'s** *to words that show belonging.*

 **Organization**   A bold beginning makes the reader want to read more.

A. Read each set of beginnings. Mark an **X** by the bold beginning.

1. _____ a. My cat's four kittens were born on my birthday.

_____ b. "Come to the barn," Alex called to me. "You have four birthday surprises!"

2. _____ a. It rained on my friend's picnic.

_____ b. Crash! Boom! Thunder rolled as we left for the picnic.

3. _____ a. Can you imagine living over a month without sunlight?

_____ b. Near the top of the world, the sky stays dark for a long time.

4. _____ a. Our family gave Gina a surprise.

_____ b. Gina's face turned three shades of red when we yelled, "Surprise!"

B. Write a bold beginning for a story about your birthday. Use sound words.

_____

_____

 **Organization**   A strong middle tells more about the story.

A. Read the story. Underline the middle sentences that tell more
   about the story. Then circle the first and last sentences.
   Add the missing apostrophes.

A Family Stroll

   "Do you want to go for a walk?" asked my mother
one morning. First, we walked past the fire station. The
firefighters were cleaning their trucks. Next, we walked
past my friends house. We waved to his family. Then, we
took another street to my grandmothers house. She was
waiting for us with a big pancake breakfast!

B. Read the beginning and ending. Then write a strong middle.

   "Come quick!" yelled Maria. "You won't believe it!"

_____

_____

_____

_____

_____

That was the best school day ever!

Organization An excellent ending brings the story together.

A. Read the story. Fix the mistake in one sentence.
   Then choose an ending from the box and circle it.

Bird Watching

One day, Grandma said, "Let's go to the park!" We packed a lunch. We found Grandma field glasses. Grandma took us to watch birds. We learned their names. We learned about nests. We found out what birds like to eat. We saw five kinds of water birds.

Possible Endings
1. **Tell what was said:** Grandma said, "You are good bird watchers."
2. **Make it funny:** Now we're bird brains!
3. **Tie it up:** Now we are expert bird watchers.

B. Write an ending for this story. Make it bring the story together.
   Fix the mistake in one sentence.

Birdhouse

Grandpa picked me up after school. We made a birdhouse. I used Grandpa tools. Grandpa helped me measure and cut the wood. Next, we nailed it together. Then, we painted the birdhouse blue because that's my favorite color.

_____

_____

Organization   Write a bold beginning, a strong middle, and an excellent ending.

Tell about a fun time you've had with your family. Draw pictures to show the beginning, middle, and ending. Then write some important words to go with your pictures.

Beginning

_____

_____

_____

_____

Middle

_____

_____

_____

Ending

_____

_____

_____

_____

DAY 1

Read the rule aloud. Then say: *Think about how you organize your things in a backpack. If items are grouped into compartments in a backpack, they are easier to find. It's the same when we write. When we group details together, they are easier to find and understand.* Then guide students through the activities.

- **Activity A:** Read the paragraph in Activity A together. Ask: *What are Cody's three groups of details?* (saving, spending, giving)

- **Activity B:** Have students identify each group of details. Then say: *The different ways you marked the sentences help you see the organization of details. What do you notice?* (The different kinds of details are grouped together.) *Grouping the details makes them easier to read.*

- **Activity C:** Say: *Let's add one detail to Cody's paragraph. It should be about saving, spending, or giving.* Have students draw and label their ideas. Invite volunteers to share their ideas.

Convention: Review end punctuation marks. Have students find and circle an example of each end mark in the paragraph.

DAY 2

Read the rule aloud. Then guide students through the activities.

- **Activity A:** Make sure students understand what can be bought at a farmer's market and a hardware store. Read the first sentence together and ask: *Where do you buy apples—the farmer's market or the hardware store?* (market) Have students write **1** on the line. Repeat the process for the remaining sentences.

- **Convention:** Say: *Now look at the list of sentences. What's missing?* (end marks) Guide students as a class to add the missing punctuation marks.

- **Activity B:** Say: *Let's add another detail to each group.* Ask: *What else can you buy at a farmer's market? A hardware store?*

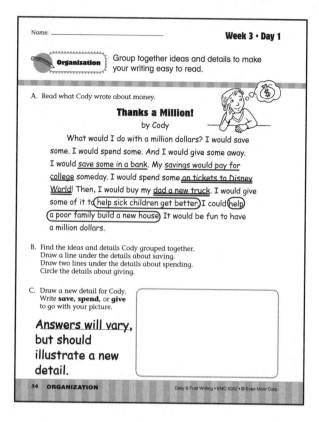

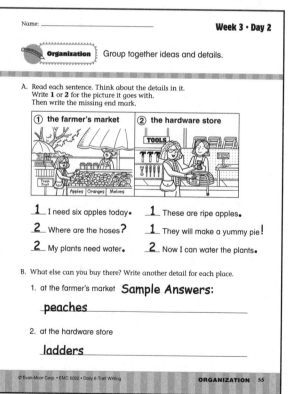

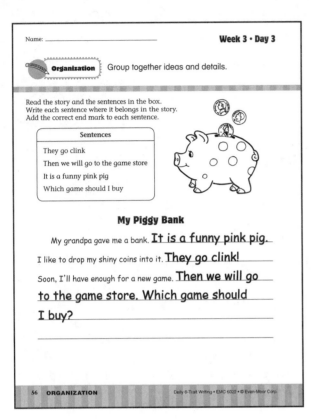

Name: _____ Week 3 • Day 3

Organization Group together ideas and details.

Read the story and the sentences in the box.
Write each sentence where it belongs in the story.
Add the correct end mark to each sentence.

Sentences
They go clink
Then we will go to the game store
It is a funny pink pig
Which game should I buy

My Piggy Bank

My grandpa gave me a bank. **It is a funny pink pig.**

I like to drop my shiny coins into it. **They go clink!**

Soon, I'll have enough for a new game. **Then we will go**

to the game store. Which game should

I buy?

_____

56 ORGANIZATION   Daily 6-Trait Writing • EMC 6022 • © Evan-Moor Corp.

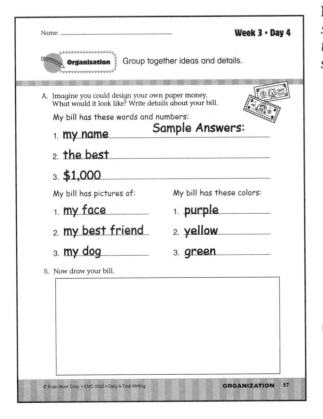

Name: _____ Week 3 • Day 4

Organization Group together ideas and details.

A. Imagine you could design your own paper money.
What would it look like? Write details about your bill.

My bill has these words and numbers:

Sample Answers:

1. **my name**
2. **the best**
3. **$1,000**

My bill has pictures of:

1. **my face**
2. **my best friend**
3. **my dog**

My bill has these colors:

1. **purple**
2. **yellow**
3. **green**

B. Now draw your bill.

© Evan-Moor Corp. • EMC 6022 • Daily 6-Trait Writing   ORGANIZATION 57

DAY 3

Review the rule. Model how to group details together. For example, write this sentence on the board: *Dad and I went to the bank.* Then ask students to decide which of the following sentences has a detail that goes with the first sentence: *1) He filled up the gas tank, or 2) He put money into his bank account.* (2) Ask: *Why does it fit?* (Because it is something you do at a bank.) Then guide students through the activity.

- Read the details and the story aloud. Ask students to choose a detail that fits as a second sentence for the story. Then ask: *Why does that sentence fit?* (It is a detail about the piggy bank.) Guide students through the remaining sentences.

Convention: Remind students to add the correct end mark to each detail sentence. Have volunteers read aloud their completed paragraphs with expression to check their answers.

DAY 4

Review the rule. Then say: *Presidents, kings, and queens sometimes have coins and bills made with their pictures on them. Imagine if you had your own money!* Then guide students through the activities.

- **Activity A:** Help students brainstorm ideas. Say: *Let's add some details to these sentences.* Ask: *What words and numbers would you put on your paper money?* (name, dollar amount) *What pictures could be on your money?* (their photo, school) *What colors would your money be?* Circulate and help students complete the activity. Then say: *Notice how all of your ideas and details are grouped together.*

- **Activity B:** Say: *Now that you've decided on your details, draw a picture of your money!* Have volunteers share their drawings and details.

DAY 5 *Writing Prompt*

- *Use your ideas and details from Day 4 to write a description of your paper money. Group together your ideas and details.*

- *Be sure to use correct end marks.*

Organization   Group together ideas and details to make your writing easy to read.

A. Read what Cody wrote about money.

Thanks a Million!

by Cody

What would I do with a million dollars? I would save some. I would spend some. And I would give some away. I would save some in a bank. My savings would pay for college someday. I would spend some on tickets to Disney World! Then, I would buy my dad a new truck. I would give some of it to help sick children get better. I could help a poor family build a new house. It would be fun to have a million dollars.

B. Find the ideas and details Cody grouped together.
Draw a line under the details about saving.
Draw two lines under the details about spending.
Circle the details about giving.

C. Draw a new detail for Cody.
Write **save**, **spend**, or **give**
to go with your picture.

_____

Organization : Group together ideas and details.

A. Read each sentence. Think about the details in it.
Write **1** or **2** for the picture it goes with.
Then write the missing end mark.

_____ I need six apples today   _____ These are ripe apples

_____ Where are the hoses   _____ They will make a yummy pie

_____ My plants need water   _____ Now I can water the plants

B. What else can you buy there? Write another detail for each place.

1. at the farmer's market

   _____

2. at the hardware store

   _____

Organization : Group together ideas and details.

Read the story and the sentences in the box.
Write each sentence where it belongs in the story.
Add the correct end mark to each sentence.

Sentences
They go clink
Then we will go to the game store
It is a funny pink pig
Which game should I buy

My Piggy Bank

My grandpa gave me a bank. _____

I like to drop my shiny coins into it. _____

Soon, I'll have enough for a new game. _____

_____

_____

_____

Organization   Group together ideas and details.

A. Imagine you could design your own paper money.
   What would it look like? Write details about your bill.

My bill has these words and numbers:

1. _____

2. _____

3. _____

My bill has pictures of: My bill has these colors:

1. _____   1. _____

2. _____   2. _____

3. _____   3. _____

B. Now draw your bill.

DAY 1

Read the rule aloud. Then ask your students to tell how a student's desk and the teacher's desk are the same and how they are different. Write students' ideas on the board in two columns. (e.g., same: used for writing, have four legs; different: one is bigger, made of different materials) Then say: *One way to organize our writing is to tell how things are the same or different.* Then guide students through the activities.

- **Activities A and B:** Read aloud the sentences. Point out that both sentences tell about soccer and baseball. Have students underline what things are the same (soccer, baseball) and what are different. (soccer, baseball; kick, hit)

- **Activity C:** Read the sentence for the first picture aloud. Say: *Look at the picture. Do the sentence and picture tell how the girls are the same or different? Circle your answer.* Repeat for the other sentence and picture.

- **Activity D (Convention):** Say: *Look again at the picture of the boys. We can write another sentence about how they are different.* Write this sentence on the board: *Tyler has a mitt, but Jerome has a bat.* Then say: *You can use a comma and the word* **but** *to tell how things are different.* Have students copy the sentence or write their own using **but**.

DAY 2

Read the rule aloud. Then say: *To group by how things are different, you have to organize your ideas and details.* Guide students through the activities.

- **Activity A:** Activate students' prior knowledge about swimming and ice-skating, focusing on where the sports take place, what equipment is used, etc. Then have students read the words in the box and look at the chart. Ask: *What are the first things listed in the chart?* (pool, rink) *Why are they listed in different columns?* (Because swimming is done in a pool, and skating is done at a rink.) Have students complete the rest of the chart, using the words in the box.

- **Activity B (Convention):** Ask: *What can you use in a sentence to compare two things?* (comma and **but**) Say: *Add a comma and the word* **but** *where they belong in the sentence.*

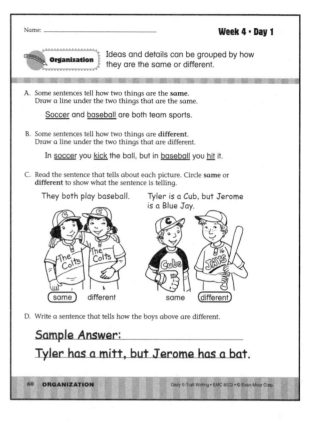

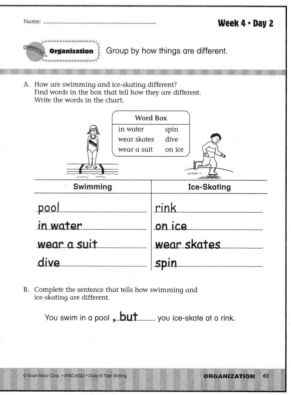

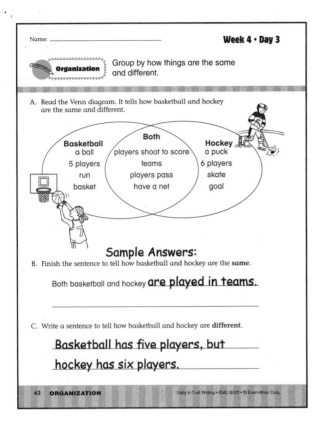

Name: _____ Week 4 • Day 3

Organization — Group by how things are the same and different.

A. Read the Venn diagram. It tells how basketball and hockey are the same and different.

Basketball
a ball
5 players
run
basket

Both
players shoot to score
teams
players pass
have a net

Hockey
a puck
6 players
skate
goal

Sample Answers:

B. Finish the sentence to tell how basketball and hockey are the **same**.

Both basketball and hockey **are played in teams.**

C. Write a sentence to tell how basketball and hockey are **different**.

Basketball has five players, but hockey has six players.

62 ORGANIZATION   Daily 6-Trait Writing • EMC 6022 • © Evan-Moor Corp.

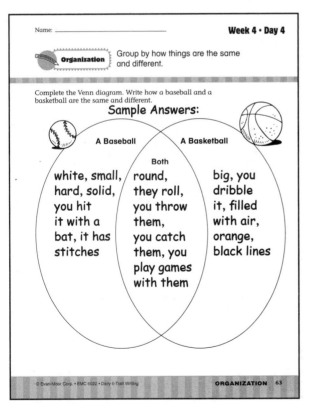

Name: _____ Week 4 • Day 4

Organization — Group by how things are the same and different.

Complete the Venn diagram. Write how a baseball and a basketball are the same and different.

Sample Answers:

A Baseball
white, small, hard, solid, you hit it with a bat, it has stitches

Both
round, they roll, you throw them, you catch them, you play games with them

A Basketball
big, you dribble it, filled with air, orange, black lines

© Evan-Moor Corp. • EMC 6022 • Daily 6-Trait Writing   ORGANIZATION 63

DAY 3

Read the rule aloud. Then guide students through the activities.

- **Activity A:** Familiarize students with the concept of a Venn diagram. Say: *In this diagram, each circle stands for a sport. Where they overlap is how the two sports are the same. The rest of each circle is how they are different.* Read the Venn diagram together and confirm students' understanding of how it shows differences and similarities between basketball and hockey.

- **Activity B:** Have students complete the sentence. If necessary, model a completed sentence. (e.g., Both basketball and hockey players shoot to score.) Invite students to share their sentences.

- **Activity C (Convention):** Have students write the sentence. Make sure they use a comma and the word **but** to compare basketball and hockey. Ask volunteers to share their sentences.

DAY 4

Review the rule. First, review the concept of a Venn diagram. Then guide students through the activity.

- Have students look at the illustrations on the page. Ask: *How could you describe the baseball? The basketball? What else do you know about each kind of ball?*

- Have students work in small groups to complete their diagrams. Then have the groups share their ideas. Allow students to make additions or changes to their diagrams, based on the ideas shared.

DAY 5 *Writing Prompt*

- *Use your ideas from Day 4 to write sentences that tell how a baseball and a basketball are the same and different.*

- *Be sure to use a comma and the word* **but** *correctly.*

Organization   Ideas and details can be grouped by how they are the same or different.

A. Some sentences tell how two things are the **same**.
Draw a line under the two things that are the same.

Soccer and baseball are both team sports.

B. Some sentences tell how two things are **different**.
Draw a line under the two things that are different.

In soccer you kick the ball, but in baseball you hit it.

C. Read the sentence that tells about each picture. Circle **same** or **different** to show what the sentence is telling.

They both play baseball.   Tyler is a Cub, but Jerome is a Blue Jay.

same   different   same   different

D. Write a sentence that tells how the boys above are different.

_____

_____

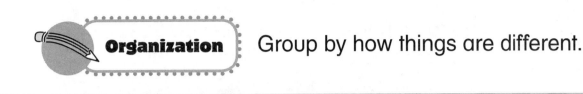

Organization Group by how things are different.

A. How are swimming and ice-skating different?
   Find words in the box that tell how they are different.
   Write the words in the chart.

Word Box

in water	spin
wear skates	dive
wear a suit	on ice

Swimming	**Ice-Skating**
pool	rink

B. Complete the sentence that tells how swimming and
   ice-skating are different.

   You swim in a pool _____ you ice-skate at a rink.

Organization

Group by how things are the same and different.

A. Read the Venn diagram. It tells how basketball and hockey are the same and different.

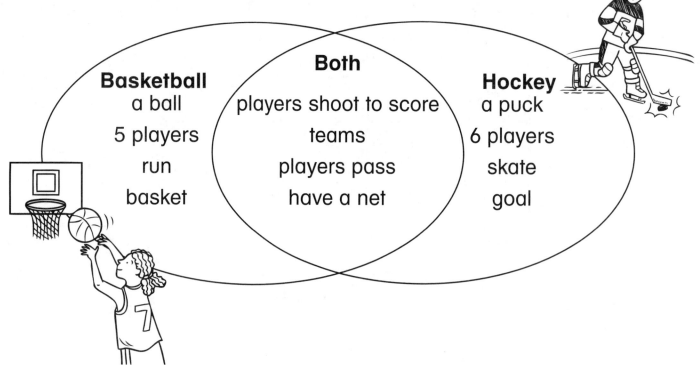

Basketball
a ball
5 players
run
basket

Both
players shoot to score
teams
players pass
have a net

Hockey
a puck
6 players
skate
goal

B. Finish the sentence to tell how basketball and hockey are the **same**.

Both basketball and hockey _____

_____

C. Write a sentence to tell how basketball and hockey are **different**.

_____

_____

Daily 6-Trait Writing • EMC 6022 • © Evan-Moor Corp.

 **Organization** Group by how things are the same and different.

Complete the Venn diagram. Write how a baseball and a basketball are the same and different.

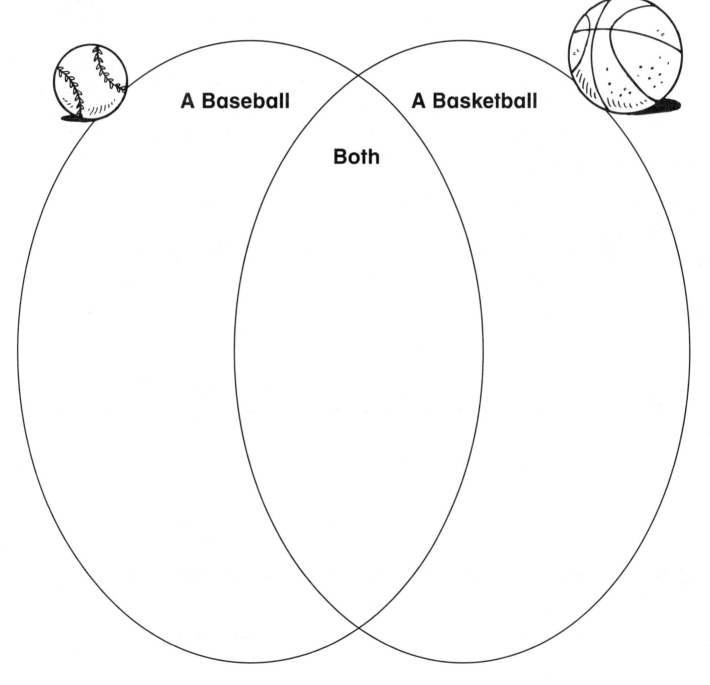

A Baseball

A Basketball

Both

DAY 1

Read the rule aloud. Remind students that a writer must put things in the right order so the reader can understand the writing. Then guide students through the activities.

- **Activity A:** Help students recall the story of "The Ugly Duckling." (A mother duck hatches eggs, but one duckling is ugly. He runs away. No one wants him. In the spring, two beautiful swans swim to him. He discovers he is a beautiful swan, too!) Then read together the instructions for making a puppet about the story. Ask: *What if you glued before drawing?* (It might be harder to draw if the glue was wet.) Say: *The steps have to be in order.*

- **Activity B:** Say: *These pictures illustrate the paragraph, but they are out of order!* Ask: *Which picture shows the first step? Let's write the word* **first** *on the line.* Continue with the remaining pictures, using **next**, **then**, and **last**. Then have students name and write action words that describe what is happening in each picture.

Convention: Say: *Use the verb* **is** *when writing about one person or thing. For example, "The student* **is** *making a puppet." Use* **are** *when writing about more than one. For example, "The students* **are** *making puppets."* Then have students tell you the correct verb to use in these sentences: *The little puppet ___ mine.* (**is**) *Their puppets ___ very colorful.* (**are**)

DAY 2

Read the rule aloud. Say: *Remember, a story should have a bold beginning, a strong middle, and an excellent ending.* Then guide students through the activity.

- Have students identify which pictures illustrate the beginning, middle, and end of the story. Then say: *Let's write our own version of this story!* Guide students to write a bold beginning sentence with quotations, sound words, questions, or details.

- Guide students to write a strong middle sentence that tells more about the story. Then help students write an ending sentence that tells what was said, uses humor, or ties up loose ends.

Convention: Have students read aloud their writing. Reinforce the correct usage of **is** and **are**.

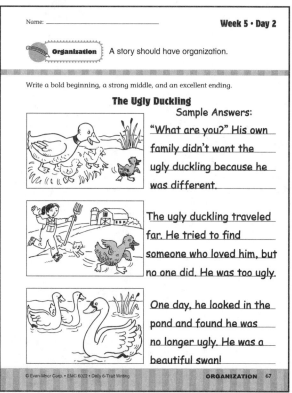

Name: _____   **Week 5 • Day 3**

Organization Group together ideas and details.

A. Read the paragraph and the sentences in the box.
Write each detail sentence where it belongs.

Sentences
It cracks open the egg.
The feathers are also wet and sticky.
The dull gray feathers will turn to snow white.

The Real Ugly Duckling

A cygnet is a name for a baby swan. A cygnet ~~are~~ *is* a bird, so

it begins life inside an egg. When it is ready to be born, the cygnet

uses its beak. It cracks open the egg. _____

A newborn cygnet's feathers ~~is~~ *are* gray. The feathers are

also wet and sticky. _____ As the cygnet

grows older, its gray feathers will change color. The dull

gray feathers will turn to snow white.

_____

B. Read the paragraph again. Use proofreading marks to correct
the use of **is** and **are**.

68 ORGANIZATION   Daily 6-Trait Writing • EMC 6022 • © Evan-Moor Corp.

Name: _____   **Week 5 • Day 4**

Organization Group by how things are the same or different.

What did you look like as a baby?
What do you look like now?
Fill in the diagram.

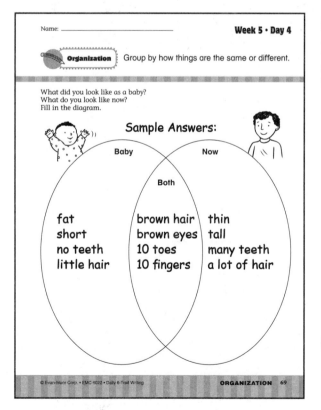

Sample Answers:

Baby | Both | Now

fat / short / no teeth / little hair   brown hair / brown eyes / 10 toes / 10 fingers   thin / tall / many teeth / a lot of hair

© Evan-Moor Corp. • EMC 6022 • Daily 6-Trait Writing   **ORGANIZATION** 69

Read the rule aloud. Then guide students through the activity.

• Before you read the paragraph or sentences, write the word **cygnet** on the board and pronounce it. Have students repeat after you. Say: *We are going to learn what this word means.*

• **Activity A:** Read the paragraph aloud. Then say: *Now let's read the sentences that will complete the paragraph.* Read the sentences aloud. Then instruct students to write the sentences in order in the paragraph. Have a volunteer read the completed paragraph aloud. Ask: *Are these sentences in order? Are the details grouped together?*

• **Activity B (Convention):** Read the paragraph again. When you finish, say: *Some of these words don't sound right. What's wrong with them?* (**Is** and **are** are used incorrectly.) Model how to use proofreading marks to correct the words. Have students find and correct the words on their papers.

Read the rule aloud. Then say: *Just as swans look different as babies, so do people!* Guide students through the activity.

• On the board, draw and explain a Venn diagram like the one on the student page. For example, say: *When I was a baby, I was bald, tiny, and wrinkly. Now I am tall and have long hair. But I still have blue eyes.* Model writing these details in the appropriate sections of the diagram. Then circulate to help students fill in their own diagrams.

• Model several ways students can construct sentences from the diagram. (e.g., "When I was a baby, I was bald. Now I have long hair. I used to be very tiny, but now I am tall.")

DAY 5 *Writing Prompt*

• *Use your diagram from Day 4 to write sentences about how you looked as a baby and how you look now. Remember to group your details.*

• *Be sure to use* **is** *and* **are** *correctly.*

Organization   Organization is putting things in the right order.

A. Read how to make a puppet.

Ugly Duckling Puppet

   Make a puppet to tell the story. First, cut two pieces of paper the same size. Next, draw the ugly duckling on one. Then, draw the beautiful swan on the other. Last, glue the pictures to a craft stick. Glue them on back to back. Use one side at a time when you tell the story.

B. Look at the pictures. Write an order word and an action word to describe which step each picture shows.

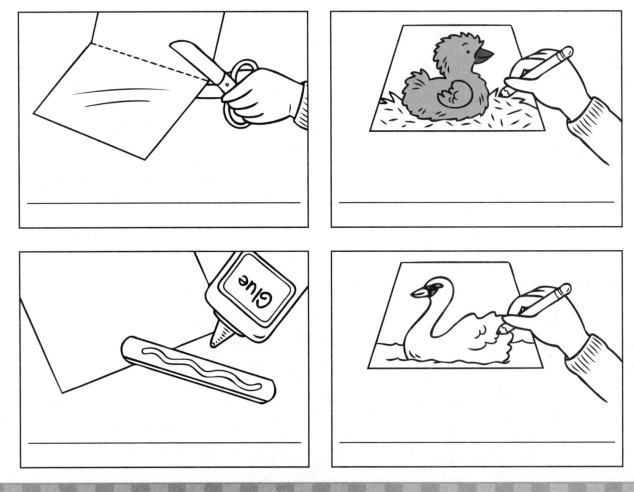

Organization) A story should have organization.

Write a bold beginning, a strong middle, and an excellent ending.

The Ugly Duckling

_____

_____

_____

_____

_____

_____

_____

_____

_____

Name: _____

Organization Group together ideas and details.

A. Read the paragraph and the sentences in the box.
Write each detail sentence where it belongs.

Sentences
It cracks open the egg.
The feathers are also wet and sticky.
The dull gray feathers will turn to snow white.

The Real Ugly Duckling

A cygnet is a name for a baby swan. A cygnet are a bird, so

it begins life inside an egg. When it is ready to be born, the cygnet

uses its beak. _____

A newborn cygnet's feathers is gray. _____

_____ As the cygnet

grows older, its gray feathers will change color. _____

_____

_____

B. Read the paragraph again. Use proofreading marks to correct
the use of **is** and **are**.

Organization Group by how things are the same or different.

What did you look like as a baby?
What do you look like now?
Fill in the diagram.

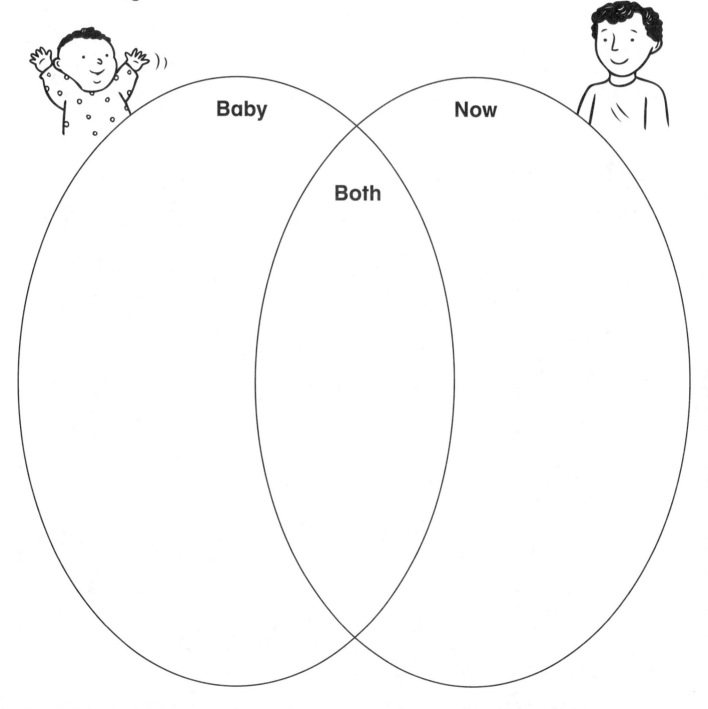

Baby

Both

Now

WORD CHOICE
Use Strong Verbs

Refer to pages 6 and 7 to introduce or review the writing trait.

DAY 1

Introduce this week's skill by saying: *Good writers choose words with care. They choose words that stand out and sparkle! Some of those words are strong verbs.*

Write the following sentences on the board and ask students to identify the verbs: *1) The Tommy Tugboat ride tilts, tips, and tosses us into the air. 2) The Tommy Tugboat ride moves like a boat.* (tilts, tips, tosses; moves) Ask: *Which sentence gives a clearer picture of the tugboat ride? Why?* (Sentence 1, because it uses exciting action words that clearly tell how the ride moves.) Read the rule aloud and guide students through the activities.

- **Activity A:** Direct students to the first picture. Ask: *Which verb under the picture is the stronger one? Which one tells more clearly what you see in the picture?* (**twirl**) Say: *Dance can mean many things, such as jump, leap, or kick. Twirl tells one specific thing the dancer is doing in the picture.*

- **Activity B (Convention):** Say: *A plural noun names more than one person, place, or thing. Some plural nouns have special spellings, such as* **children***.* Direct students to read the sentences, underline the strong verbs, and circle the plural nouns. Point out that they are different from many other plurals because they do not end in **s** or **es**.

DAY 2

Read the rule aloud. Then read the following sentences and have students identify the verbs: *Mother will get me a hat. Mother will buy me a hat.* (**get, buy**) Ask: *Which verb gives a clearer picture of what Mother will do?* (**buy**) Say: *The word* **buy** *is more clear. It tells exactly what Mother will do. Using stronger verbs instead of words like* **get** *and* **go** *makes your writing more clear.*

- **Activity A:** For item 1, ask: *Which verb is more clear,* **go** *or* **start**? (**start**) *Start tells exactly what the tractor won't do.* Guide students to complete the other items individually. Have volunteers read their completed sentences aloud to check the answers and reinforce the lesson.

- **Activity B (Convention):** Remind students that some plural nouns have special spellings. Have students search Activity A to find the irregular plural nouns that match the descriptions in Activity B.

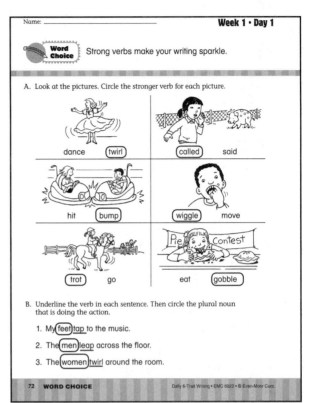

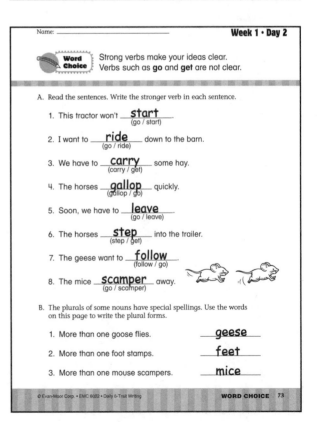

Name: _____ **Week 1 • Day 3**

Word Choice Strong verbs make your writing interesting.
Use verbs that aren't "tired."

A. Read the story below. The underlined words are "tired" verbs.
Find a stronger verb to use instead. Write each tired verb next
to a strong verb in the chart.

At the Fair

The fair had a watermelon-eating contest. My brother
and I <u>went</u> early and entered it. We <u>ate</u> our watermelon.
Then, my tooth <u>came</u> loose! Out it <u>came</u>! I had to stop
eating. My brother never stopped, though. He kept
chomping away. He <u>got</u> first prize!

Strong Verbs	Tired Verbs
gobbled	ate
wiggled	came
arrived	went
won	got
popped	came

B. Write a sentence about teeth. Use a strong verb from this page,
or use your own. **Sample Answer:**
My teeth wiggle when they are loose.

C. Write the plurals for **tooth** and **child** to complete the sentence.

How many teeth have the children lost?

74 WORD CHOICE — Daily 6-Trait Writing • EMC 6022 • © Evan-Moor Corp.

Name: _____ **Week 1 • Day 4**

Word Choice Use strong verbs in your writing.

Think about lunchtime at your school.
How many different ways can you eat something?
Read the verbs for **eat**. Draw a picture of a food for each one.
Then write and draw three more strong verbs.

Sample Answers:

carrots	hot dog	crackers
munch	gobble	nibble
soup	ice cream	bread
slurp	lick	chew

© Evan-Moor Corp. • EMC 6022 • Daily 6-Trait Writing — **WORD CHOICE** 75

DAY 3

Read the rule aloud. Then say: *Some writers use the
same verbs over and over again. Those verbs become
"tired"! We can make our writing more interesting by using
strong verbs instead of the tired ones.* Guide students
through the activities.

- **Activity A:** Read the story together. Then guide
students to find substitutes for the underlined
tired words. Have a volunteer read the improved
story aloud using the stronger verbs.

- **Activity B:** Have students search the page or
think of their own strong verb for their sentence.

- **Activity C (Convention):** Remind students that
some plural nouns have special spellings. Ask
one student to write the completed sentence on
the board to check and model the spelling.

DAY 4

Read the rule aloud. Then guide students through the
activity. You may want to have them work in small
groups.

- Say: *You know that using strong verbs can make your
writing clearer and more interesting. Today, think of
strong verbs that can be used instead of* **eat**. *(e.g.,*
chew, crunch, gulp, swallow, feast, snack, dine)
Say: *Three strong verbs are provided for you. Can you
think of three more? Write them in the boxes. Then
think of a food that goes with each strong verb and
draw a picture of it.*

- When students have completed their papers, have
them share their words and pictures with the
class. Confirm students' use and knowledge of
strong verbs by writing their verbs on the board.

DAY 5 *Writing Prompt*

- *Describe what lunchtime is like at your school. Use
your strong verbs from Day 4 to tell how kids eat
and act.*

- *Some plural nouns have special spellings. Be sure
to spell these words correctly.*

Word Choice   Strong verbs make your writing sparkle.

A. Look at the pictures. Circle the stronger verb for each picture.

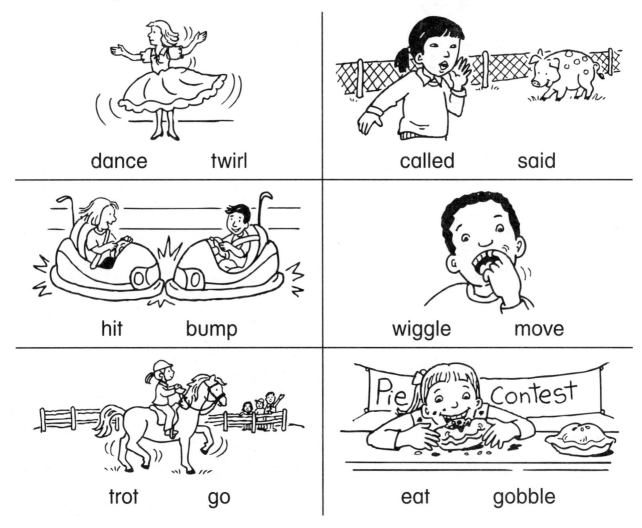

dance	twirl	called	said
hit	bump	wiggle	move
trot	go	eat	gobble

B. Underline the verb in each sentence. Then circle the plural noun that is doing the action.

1. My feet tap to the music.

2. The men leap across the floor.

3. The women twirl around the room.

 **Word Choice** — Strong verbs make your ideas clear.
Verbs such as **go** and **get** are not clear.

A. Read the sentences. Write the stronger verb in each sentence.

1. This tractor won't _____.
   (go / start)

2. I want to _____ down to the barn.
   (go / ride)

3. We have to _____ some hay.
   (carry / get)

4. The horses _____ quickly.
   (gallop / go)

5. Soon, we have to _____.
   (go / leave)

6. The horses _____ into the trailer.
   (step / get)

7. The geese want to _____.
   (follow / go)

8. The mice _____ away.
   (go / scamper)

B. The plurals of some nouns have special spellings. Use the words on this page to write the plural forms.

1. More than one goose flies.   _____

2. More than one foot stamps.   _____

3. More than one mouse scampers.   _____

Word Choice

Strong verbs make your writing interesting.
Use verbs that aren't "tired."

A. Read the story below. The underlined words are "tired" verbs.
Find a stronger verb to use instead. Write each tired verb next
to a strong verb in the chart.

At the Fair

The fair had a watermelon-eating contest. My brother
and I <u>went</u> early and entered it. We <u>ate</u> our watermelon.
Then, my tooth <u>came</u> loose! Out it <u>came</u>! I had to stop
eating. My brother never stopped, though. He kept
chomping away. He <u>got</u> first prize!

Strong Verbs	Tired Verbs
gobbled	_____
wiggled	_____
arrived	_____
won	_____
popped	_____

B. Write a sentence about teeth. Use a strong verb from this page,
or use your own.

_____

C. Write the plurals for **tooth** and **child** to complete the sentence.

How many _____ have the _____ lost?

Word Choice   Use strong verbs in your writing.

Think about lunchtime at your school.
How many different ways can you eat something?
Read the verbs for **eat**. Draw a picture of a food for each one.
Then write and draw three more strong verbs.

munch   gobble   nibble

WORD CHOICE
Describe the Action

DAY 1

Say: *Good writers describe action by using words called adverbs. Adverbs tell more about the action. They can tell **how** something happens and add meaning to a sentence. Adverbs that tell **how** often end with the letters **ly**.*

Say: *The train chugged up the long hill.* Then ask: ***How could the train chug up the long hill?*** Use the responses to create sentences. (e.g., *The train chugged **slowly** up the long hill.*) Point out that by adding the adverb, the meaning of the sentence became more clear. Then read the rule aloud. Guide students through the activities.

- **Activity A:** Have students look at the first picture and read the verb. Ask: *Is the woman singing loudly or neatly?* (**loudly**) *Loudly best describes the action.* Repeat for the other pictures.

- **Activity B:** Ask: *What are some adverbs that could complete the first sentence?* Write them on the board. Then have students choose one to write. Repeat with sentence 2.

Convention: Say: *Days of the week begin with a capital letter.* Then ask students to circle the capital letter in each day of the week. (**Friday, Tuesday**)

DAY 2

Read the rule aloud. Say: *We learned that we can use adverbs in our writing to tell **how** an action is done. Adverbs can also tell **when** or **where** an action takes place.*

Write the following sentences on the board: *1) The children go to bed late. 2) I like to read upstairs.* Help students identify the adverbs by asking: *Which word tells **when**?* (**late**) Ask: *Which word tells **where**?* (**upstairs**) Then guide students through the activities.

- **Activity A:** Ask: *What actions are taking place in this picture?* (e.g., snowing, building, sliding) Read the word pairs in the box together and guide students to determine in which sentence they belong. Then have students circle the adverb in each completed sentence. Read the completed sentences and have students say whether each tells **how**, **when**, or **where**. (how, when, when, where)

- **Activity B (Convention):** Write the days of the week on the board. Remind students that each one begins with a capital letter. Then have students complete the activity.

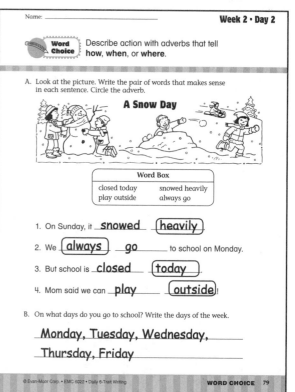

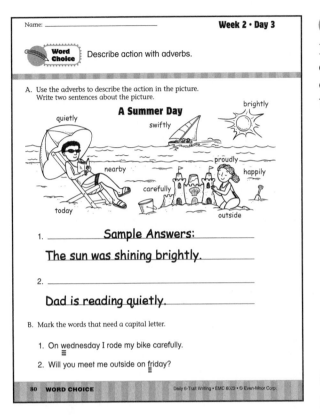

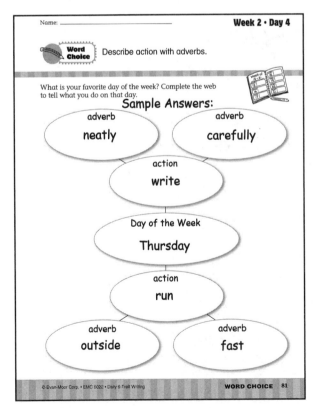

Read the rule aloud. Remind students that they can use adverbs in their writing to tell **how**, **when**, or **where** the action happens. Then guide students through the activities.

- **Activity A:** Have students tell about the actions they see in the picture. (e.g., Dad reading, child playing, boat sailing, sun shining) Then have volunteers read the words in the picture and use them in sentences. (e.g., The child is playing happily in the sand. A boat swiftly sails out to sea.) Have students write two sentences that describe the actions.

- **Activity B (Convention):** Have students use proofreading marks to indicate which words should be capitalized. (**Wednesday** and **Friday**) Model using the marks, if necessary.

Read the rule aloud. Then guide students through the activity.

- Say: *We've learned that it's important to describe action. Let's use this web to plan our ideas about what we do on our favorite day.*

- Ask prompting questions to help students complete the web: *What's your favorite day of the week?* (e.g., Saturday) *Why? What two things do you do on that day?* (e.g., dance, play sports) *How can you tell more about what you do?* (use adverbs) Then say: *Write two adverbs that tell **how, when**, or **where** you do each thing.* (e.g., gracefully, happily; outside, quietly) Have students share their ideas.

Writing Prompt

- *Write a description of what you do on your favorite day of the week. Use your web from Day 4. Remember to use adverbs to describe action.*

- *Be sure to capitalize the day of the week you are writing about.*

 **Word Choice** Adverbs describe action.
Some adverbs tell **how**.

A. Circle the adverb that goes with the picture.

sing   loudly   neatly

run   swiftly   tightly

act   carefully   kindly

talk   secretly   finally

B. Finish each sentence with an adverb that describes the action.
Underline the word that names a day of the week.

1. Kyra ran _____ in the race on Friday.

2. Tim sang _____ in music class on Tuesday.

Name: _____

 **Word Choice** Describe action with adverbs that tell **how**, **when**, or **where**.

A. Look at the picture. Write the pair of words that makes sense in each sentence. Circle the adverb.

A Snow Day

Word Box	
closed today	snowed heavily
play outside	always go

1. On Sunday, it _____ _____.

2. We _____ _____ to school on Monday.

3. But school is _____ _____.

4. Mom said we can _____ _____!

B. On what days do you go to school? Write the days of the week.

_____

_____

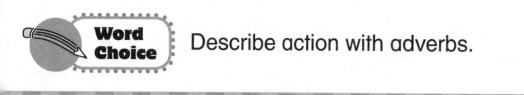

Word Choice   Describe action with adverbs.

A. Use the adverbs to describe the action in the picture.
   Write two sentences about the picture.

A Summer Day

brightly

quietly

swiftly

nearby

proudly

happily

carefully

today

outside

1. _____

   _____

2. _____

   _____

B. Mark the words that need a capital letter.

   1. On wednesday I rode my bike carefully.

   2. Will you meet me outside on friday?

Word Choice   Describe action with adverbs.

What is your favorite day of the week? Complete the web to tell what you do on that day.

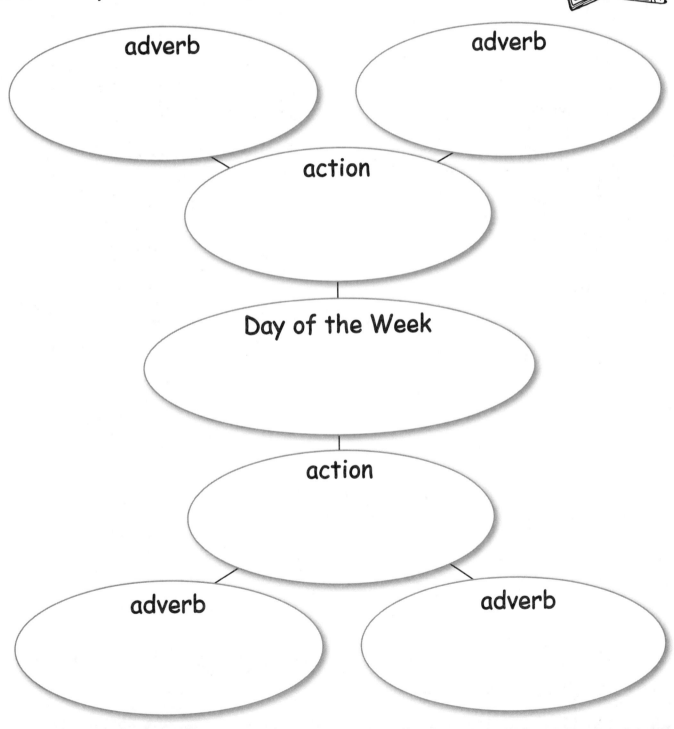

adverb

adverb

action

Day of the Week

action

adverb

adverb

DAY 1

Read the rule aloud. Then say: *Describing words can tell what color, size, or shape something is, or how many there are. For example,* **blue, little, bumpy,** *and* **ten** *are describing words.* Choose an object in the classroom and ask students to use describing words to tell more about it. (e.g., pencil: yellow, sharp, long) Then guide students through the activities.

- **Activity A:** Direct students to look at the pictures of the dinosaur and the bird. Then read the words in the box together. Ask: *Does the word* **tiny** *describe the dinosaur or the bird?* Have students write it under the correct picture. Say: *Tiny describes the size of the bird.* Repeat the process with the remaining words.

- **Activity B:** Have students write their own describing word to describe the dinosaur and bird. If necessary, brainstorm as a class.

DAY 2

Read the rule aloud. Then say: *Describing words that tell about people, places, and things are called* **adjectives.** *Writers use adjectives to give a clearer idea about someone or something.* Read the following examples and ask students to picture them in their minds: *1) Walker found a rock. 2) Walker found a pointy black rock.* Ask: *Did the sentences create different pictures in your mind? How were they different?* (e.g., Students may have pictured a round pebble for the first sentence.) Say: *That's an example of how adjectives make ideas clear. Without the adjectives, you could picture something different.* Then guide students through the activities.

- **Activity A:** Read sentence 1 aloud and ask: *Which word is an adjective,* **under** *or* **red**? *(red)* **Red** *is an adjective because it tells more about the rocks. It tells what color the rocks are.* Repeat the process for sentences 2 through 6.

- **Activity B (Convention):** Review contractions. Say: *Contractions are a short way of writing two words. Use an apostrophe to take the place of a missing letter or letters.* Model how a contraction is formed with the word **don't.** (do not = don't) Then ask students to find and circle the three contractions on the page and complete the activity.

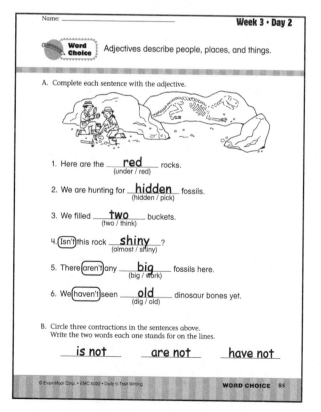

Daily 6-Trait Writing • EMC 6022 • © Evan-Moor Corp.

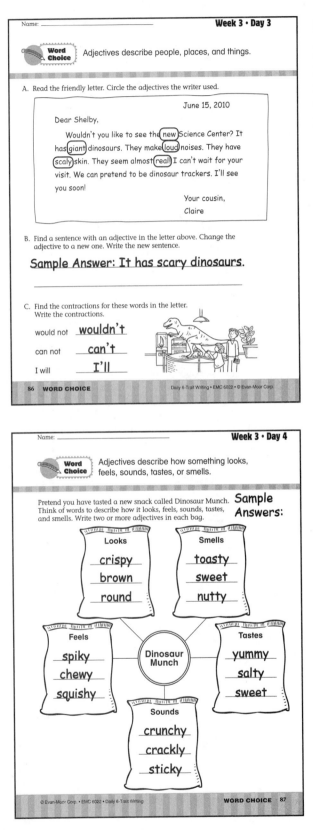

Week 3 • Day 3

Name: _____

Word Choice Adjectives describe people, places, and things.

A. Read the friendly letter. Circle the adjectives the writer used.

June 15, 2010

Dear Shelby,

Wouldn't you like to see the (new) Science Center? It has (giant) dinosaurs. They make (loud) noises. They have (scaly) skin. They seem almost (real) I can't wait for your visit. We can pretend to be dinosaur trackers. I'll see you soon!

Your cousin,
Claire

B. Find a sentence with an adjective in the letter above. Change the adjective to a new one. Write the new sentence.

Sample Answer: It has scary dinosaurs.

_____

C. Find the contractions for these words in the letter. Write the contractions.

would not   **wouldn't**

can not   **can't**

I will   **I'll**

86 WORD CHOICE   Daily 6-Trait Writing • EMC 6022 • © Evan-Moor Corp.

Week 3 • Day 4

Name: _____

Word Choice Adjectives describe how something looks, feels, sounds, tastes, or smells.

Pretend you have tasted a new snack called Dinosaur Munch. Think of words to describe how it looks, feels, sounds, tastes, and smells. Write two or more adjectives in each bag.

Sample Answers:

Looks
crispy
brown
round

Smells
toasty
sweet
nutty

Feels
spiky
chewy
squishy

Dinosaur Munch

Tastes
yummy
salty
sweet

Sounds
crunchy
crackly
sticky

© Evan-Moor Corp. • EMC 6022 • Daily 6-Trait Writing   WORD CHOICE 87

Review the rule. Then use the letter to Shelby to review the elements of a friendly letter: heading (date), greeting (Dear Shelby,), body, closing (Your cousin,), and signature. Have students point to each part as you name it. Then guide students through the activities.

- **Activity A:** Begin reading the letter aloud. To check for skill acquisition, have students raise their hands when you come to an adjective. Stop and give students time to circle the adjective. Continue through the letter.

- **Activity B:** Write the following sentence on the board and invite students to name the adjective: *This dinosaur had a long tail.* (**long**) Then have them think of a different adjective and restate the sentence. (e.g., This dinosaur had a spiky tail.) Instruct students to choose another sentence from the letter and rewrite it using a new adjective.

- **Activity C (Convention):** Remind students of the definition of a contraction. Then provide students with word pairs such as **is not**, **are not**, and **have not** and challenge students to form contractions with them. (e.g., **isn't**, **aren't**, **haven't**) Then have students read the words in Activity C, find the contractions in the letter, and write them on the corresponding lines.

DAY 4

Read the rule aloud. Then guide students through the activity.

Help students brainstorm what kind of a snack Dinosaur Munch might be. (e.g., crunchy crackers, chewy fruit bites) Model filling in the graphic organizer by writing an adjective in one of the boxes. Then have students work in pairs to write two or more adjectives for each of the five categories.

DAY 5 *Writing Prompt*

- *Write a letter to a friend, telling him or her about your new favorite snack—Dinosaur Munch. Use your adjectives from Day 4 to describe the snack.*

- *Be sure to spell contractions correctly.*

Word Choice — Describing words tell more about people, places, and things.

A. Write each describing word under the correct picture.

Word Box

tiny	terrible	light	graceful
scaly	spiky	huge	feathery

_____

_____

_____

_____

_____

_____

_____

_____

B. Write your own describing word for each picture.

_____   _____

Word Choice Adjectives describe people, places, and things.

A. Complete each sentence with the adjective.

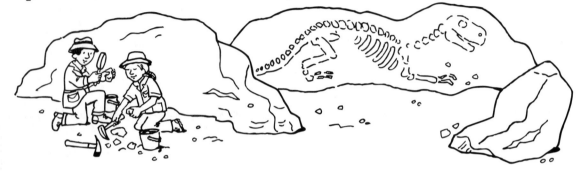

1. Here are the _____ rocks.
   (under / red)

2. We are hunting for _____ fossils.
   (hidden / pick)

3. We filled _____ buckets.
   (two / think)

4. Isn't this rock _____?
   (almost / shiny)

5. There aren't any _____ fossils here.
   (big / work)

6. We haven't seen _____ dinosaur bones yet.
   (dig / old)

B. Circle three contractions in the sentences above.
   Write the two words each one stands for on the lines.

_____   _____   _____

Word Choice   Adjectives describe people, places, and things.

A. Read the friendly letter. Circle the adjectives the writer used.

> June 15, 2010
>
> Dear Shelby,
>
> Wouldn't you like to see the new Science Center? It has giant dinosaurs. They make loud noises. They have scaly skin. They seem almost real! I can't wait for your visit. We can pretend to be dinosaur trackers. I'll see you soon!
>
> Your cousin,
> Claire

B. Find a sentence with an adjective in the letter above. Change the adjective to a new one. Write the new sentence.

_____

_____

C. Find the contractions for these words in the letter. Write the contractions.

would not   _____

can not   _____

I will   _____

Word Choice

Adjectives describe how something looks, feels, sounds, tastes, or smells.

Pretend you have tasted a new snack called Dinosaur Munch. Think of words to describe how it looks, feels, sounds, tastes, and smells. Write two or more adjectives in each bag.

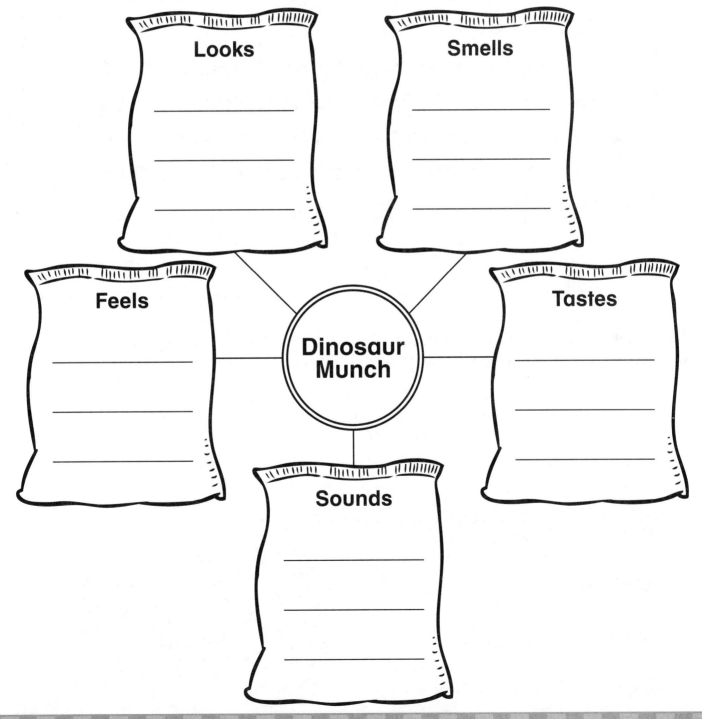

Looks

Smells

Feels

Dinosaur Munch

Tastes

Sounds

WORD CHOICE
Use Exact Nouns

DAY 1

Introduce the skill by saying: *If you give an answer in class and the teacher says you are "exactly right," what does that mean?* (The answer is correct.) *What does exact mean?* (correct, specific, just right) *Good writers choose their words carefully and use exact nouns. This means they may write* **sandal** *instead of* **shoe**, *or* **baseball cap** *instead of* **hat**. Read the rule aloud. Then guide students through the activities.

- **Activity A:** Ask students to close their eyes and listen as you read the following sentences: *My baby sister looks hilarious in Mom's shoes. My baby sister looks hilarious in Mom's high heels.* Have students tell which sentence paints a clearer picture in their mind. (the second) Ask: *What is the weak noun in the first sentence?* (shoes) *What is the exact noun?* (high heels) Then read together the pairs of sentences in the activity and have students mark the ones that use exact nouns.

- **Activity B (Convention):** Review placing a question mark at the end of an asking sentence. Have students read aloud the last sentence in Activity A. Ask: *What kind of sentence is this?* (question/asking) *What end mark should an asking sentence have?* (question mark)

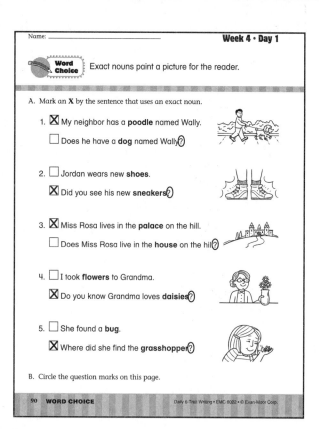

DAY 2

Read the rule aloud. Then guide students through the activities.

- **Activity A:** Say or write the following pairs of nouns and have students tell you which noun is weak and which is exact: **bike** (weak)/**BMX racer** (exact), **Oaty-Os** (exact)/**cereal** (weak). Then have students study the illustration. Read aloud the words in the word box and confirm their meanings. Then ask students to find two words that name each element of the picture. For example, **tree** and **oak**. Ask: *Which is the exact noun?* (oak) Have them write the exact noun by that picture and cross out the weak noun in the word box.

- **Activity B (Convention):** Direct students to work with a partner and ask each other questions about the picture. (e.g., Who is that man?) Then have students write one of their questions. Remind them to use the correct end mark.

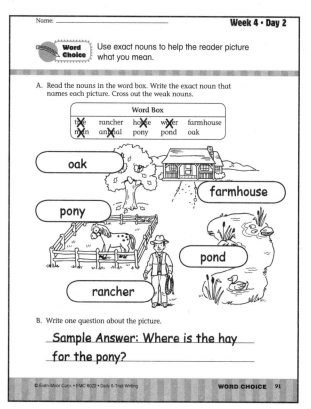

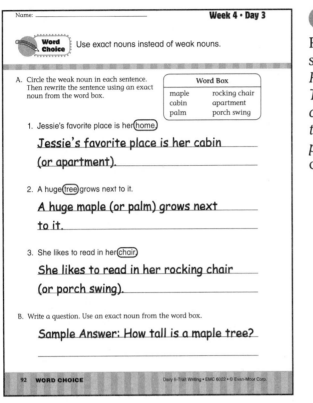

Name: _____

Word Choice Use exact nouns instead of weak nouns.

A. Circle the weak noun in each sentence. Then rewrite the sentence using an exact noun from the word box.

Word Box
maple	rocking chair
cabin	apartment
palm	porch swing

1. Jessie's favorite place is her (home).

   Jessie's favorite place is her cabin (or apartment).

2. A huge (tree) grows next to it.

   A huge maple (or palm) grows next to it.

3. She likes to read in her (chair).

   She likes to read in her rocking chair (or porch swing).

B. Write a question. Use an exact noun from the word box.

   Sample Answer: How tall is a maple tree?

92 WORD CHOICE • Daily 6-Trait Writing • EMC 6022 • © Evan-Moor Corp.

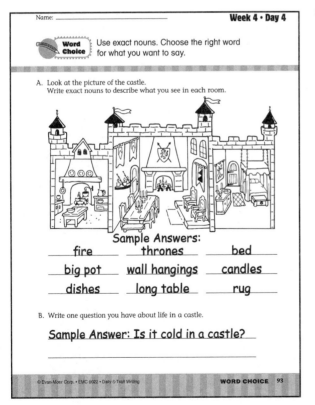

Name: _____

Word Choice Use exact nouns. Choose the right word for what you want to say.

A. Look at the picture of the castle. Write exact nouns to describe what you see in each room.

Sample Answers:
fire	thrones	bed
big pot	wall hangings	candles
dishes	long table	rug

B. Write one question you have about life in a castle.

   Sample Answer: Is it cold in a castle?

© Evan-Moor Corp. • EMC 6022 • Daily 6-Trait Writing   WORD CHOICE 93

DAY 3

Read the rule aloud. Then read or write the following sentence and ask students to identify the weak noun: *Ryan watched a bug crawl up the fence post.* (**bug**) Say: *There are many kinds of bugs. We need to tell what kind of bug Ryan watched.* Then say: *Name some exact nouns that we could use instead of **bug** in order to paint a picture for the reader.* (e.g., fly, spider, ladybug, beetle, caterpillar) Then guide students through the activities.

- **Activity A:** For sentence 1, have students circle the weak noun. (**home**) Then have them find two exact nouns that can replace it. Have students rewrite the sentence using the noun they like best. Repeat for sentences 2 and 3.

- **Activity B (Convention):** Have students draw a line under each exact noun in the box that they didn't use. Then ask: *What does an asking sentence need at the end?* (a question mark) Say: *Choose one of the nouns you just underlined and use it in a question. For example, you could write "Do you have a porch swing?"*

DAY 4

Read the rule aloud. Then guide students through the activities.

- **Activity A:** Model generating exact nouns for one of the rooms. (e.g., throne, dining table, candles, wood floor, wall hangings) Then divide students into small groups. Have each group choose a room to describe, using exact nouns. Circulate and provide vocabulary as necessary. Then have students share what they wrote.

- **Activity B (Convention):** Ask: *Based on this picture, what is one question you have about life in a castle? Write your question on the line. Be sure to use the correct end mark.*

DAY 5 *Writing Prompt*

- *Look at the picture from Day 4. Write a description of the castle. Use some of the exact nouns you wrote.*

- *Write a question at the top of your page. Be sure to place a question mark at the end.*

Word Choice   Exact nouns paint a picture for the reader.

A. Mark an **X** by the sentence that uses an exact noun.

1. ☐ My neighbor has a **poodle** named Wally.

   ☐ Does he have a **dog** named Wally?

2. ☐ Jordan wears new **shoes**.

   ☐ Did you see his new **sneakers**?

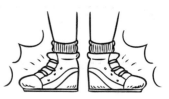

3. ☐ Miss Rosa lives in the **palace** on the hill.

   ☐ Does Miss Rosa live in the **house** on the hill?

4. ☐ I took **flowers** to Grandma.

   ☐ Do you know Grandma loves **daisies**?

5. ☐ She found a **bug**.

   ☐ Where did she find the **grasshopper**?

B. Circle the question marks on this page.

Word Choice Use exact nouns to help the reader picture what you mean.

A. Read the nouns in the word box. Write the exact noun that names each picture. Cross out the weak nouns.

Word Box				
tree	rancher	house	water	farmhouse
man	animal	pony	pond	oak

B. Write one question about the picture.

_____

_____

 **Word Choice** ⋮ Use exact nouns instead of weak nouns.

A. Circle the weak noun in each sentence. Then rewrite the sentence using an exact noun from the word box.

Word Box	
maple	rocking chair
cabin	apartment
palm	porch swing

1. Jessie's favorite place is her home.

   _____

   _____

2. A huge tree grows next to it.

   _____

   _____

3. She likes to read in her chair.

   _____

   _____

B. Write a question. Use an exact noun from the word box.

   _____

   _____

    Daily 6-Trait Writing • EMC 6022 • © Evan-Moor Corp.

Word Choice Use exact nouns. Choose the right word for what you want to say.

A. Look at the picture of the castle.
Write exact nouns to describe what you see in each room.

_____   _____   _____

_____   _____   _____

_____   _____   _____

B. Write one question you have about life in a castle.

_____

_____

DAY 1

Read the rule aloud. Say: *Remember that good writers choose words with care. They choose strong verbs over plain, weak ones. Strong verbs make your writing clearer.* Then guide students through the activities.

- **Activity A:** For the first book, ask: *What do you think this book is about?* (buried treasure) Then ask: *Which verb would be better to use if you were writing about the topic of this book—look or search? Which verb is stronger?* (**search**, because you search for buried treasure) Say: ***Look** can mean many things, but **search** has a clearer meaning.* Repeat for the remaining books.

- **Activity B (Convention):** Say: *Some verbs need helping words such as **has** or **have**. The verb **seen** needs a helping word. We must put **has** or **have** in front of **seen**.* Write these examples on the board: *I **saw** that old car in the parade. I **have seen** one like it before. Chad **has seen** it, too.* Ask: *Which word needs a helping word—**saw** or **seen**?* (**seen**) Read the sentences in the activity together, and have students underline the helping words.

DAY 2

Read the rule aloud. Review adverbs by saying: *Adverbs tell how the action is done and add meaning to a sentence. They make a sentence more clear.* Then guide students through the activities.

- **Activity A:** Read aloud the adverbs in the word box. Then read item 1 and ask: *Which adverb in the box could be used to tell how Carlos writes with care?* (neatly) Have students fill in the adverb. Repeat for items 2 through 4.

- **Activity B:** Help students brainstorm topics for their sentences. After students have written their sentences, have volunteers read them aloud.

- **Activity C (Convention):** After students have circled **saw** and **seen** in Activity A, ask them if there is a helping word in front of the words. Guide students to conclude that **seen** needs a helping word, but **saw** does not.

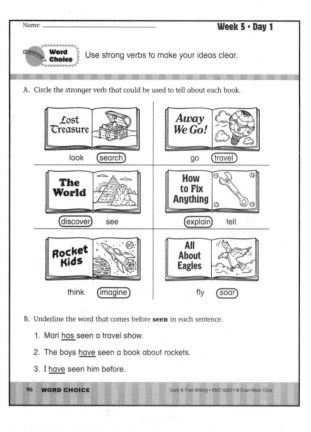

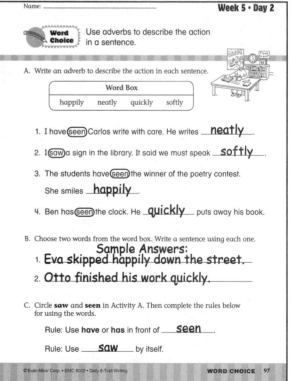

Week 5 • Day 3

Name: _____

Word Choice Use adjectives to describe people, places, and things.

A. Read the paragraph Amy wrote about her school. Circle the adjectives.

My school is in a (small) town on a (quiet) street. (Many) people make my school a (happy) place. (Kind), (smart) teachers help students learn. Cooks prepare (hot), (tasty) lunches. Cleaners scrub the floors to keep them (shiny).

B. Write two sentences to add to Amy's paragraph. Use at least one adjective in each sentence.

1. Sample Answer: The careful bus drivers keep us safe.

2. _____

Proofreading Marks:

C. Use proofreading marks to fix the sentences.

insert **has** OR delete **seen**, insert **saw**
1. Matt seen the new library.

delete **saw**, insert **seen** OR delete **have**
2. Megan and Abby have saw it, too.

delete **seen**, insert **saw** OR insert **have**
3. I seen it on my way to school.

98 **WORD CHOICE**   Daily 6-Trait Writing • EMC 6022 • © Evan-Moor Corp.

DAY 3

Read the rule aloud. Then guide students through the activities.

- **Activity A:** Read the paragraph aloud. Have students circle the adjectives on their own or in pairs. Then have a volunteer read the paragraph aloud while the rest of the class raises their hands each time they hear a circled word.

- **Activity B:** Ask: *What other details could Amy include about her school? What other people might work at her school?* (e.g., principal, nurse, bus driver, librarian) Say: *Use your imagination to write a sentence that tells more about Amy's school. Be sure to include at least one adjective in each sentence.*

- **Activity C (Convention):** Guide students to use proofreading marks to correct the usage of **saw** and **seen**. Point out that there are two correct ways to fix each sentence. Have students read their corrected sentences aloud.

Week 5 • Day 4

Name: _____

Word Choice Use exact nouns to tell just what you want to say.

Think about your school. Fill in the chart with exact nouns.

Sample Answers:

Weak Noun	Exact Noun
school	Jackson Elementary
class	2nd grade
teacher	Mr. Wong
book	Mercy Watson to the Rescue
friend	Esteban
meal	lunch
food	carrots

© Evan-Moor Corp. • EMC 6022 • Daily 6-Trait Writing   **WORD CHOICE** 99

DAY 4

Read the rule aloud. Then review: *Exact nouns paint a picture for the reader. A writer might use* **shark** *instead of* **fish**, *or* **sombrero** *in place of* **hat** *to bring different things to mind.* Then guide students through the activity.

- Say: *Let's change these weak nouns into exact nouns that tell about our own school. First, how can we make* **school** *an exact noun?* (change it to our school's name)

- Have students work individually or in pairs to complete the chart with nouns specific to your school or classroom.

DAY 5 *Writing Prompt*

- *Write a description of your school. Include exact nouns, strong verbs, adjectives, and adverbs. Use your ideas from Day 4.*

- *Be sure to use* **saw** *and* **seen** *correctly.*

 **Word Choice**   Use strong verbs to make your ideas clear.

A. Circle the stronger verb that could be used to tell about each book.

look   search

go   travel

discover   see

explain   tell

think   imagine

fly   soar

B. Underline the word that comes before **seen** in each sentence.

1. Mari has seen a travel show.

2. The boys have seen a book about rockets.

3. I have seen him before.

Word Choice Use adverbs to describe the action in a sentence.

A. Write an adverb to describe the action in each sentence.

Word Box
happily   neatly   quickly   softly

1. I have seen Carlos write with care. He writes _____.

2. I saw a sign in the library. It said we must speak _____.

3. The students have seen the winner of the poetry contest.

   She smiles _____.

4. Ben has seen the clock. He _____ puts away his book.

B. Choose two words from the word box. Write a sentence using each one.

1. _____

2. _____

C. Circle **saw** and **seen** in Activity A. Then complete the rules below for using the words.

   Rule: Use **have** or **has** in front of _____.

   Rule: Use _____ by itself.

Word Choice Use adjectives to describe people, places, and things.

A. Read the paragraph Amy wrote about her school. Circle the adjectives.

My school is in a small town on a quiet street. Many people make my school a happy place. Kind, smart teachers help students learn. Cooks prepare hot, tasty lunches. Cleaners scrub the floors to keep them shiny.

B. Write two sentences to add to Amy's paragraph. Use at least one adjective in each sentence.

1. _____

_____

2. _____

_____

C. Use proofreading marks to fix the sentences.

1. Matt seen the new library.

2. Megan and Abby have saw it, too.

3. I seen it on my way to school.

Word Choice Use exact nouns to tell just what you want to say.

Think about your school.
Fill in the chart with exact nouns.

Weak Noun	Exact Noun
school	_____
class	_____
teacher	_____
book	_____
friend	_____
meal	_____
food	_____

SENTENCE FLUENCY
Write a Sentence

Refer to pages 6 and 7 to introduce or review the writing trait.

DAY 1

Read the rule aloud. Ask: *Which of these is a complete sentence? 1) Brianna and I. 2) Brianna and I love cookies.* (2) Write the second sentence on the board. Then say: *This sentence has a naming part* (circle **Brianna and I**) *that names who or what the sentence is about. It also has a telling part* (underline **love cookies**) *that tells what the naming part does.* Then guide students through the activities. You may wish to do these as a group.

- **Activity A:** Say: *Look at the first picture.* Ask: *What is in the jug?* (milk) Say: **Milk** *is the naming part.* **Milk** *is what the sentence is about.* Then guide students through the second picture.

- **Activity B:** For the first picture, ask: *What is the baby doing?* (crawling to a bear) Work with students to craft a telling part on the board. (e.g., crawls toward the bear) Repeat for the second picture.

- **Activity C (Convention):** Say: *You use the words* **I** *and* **me** *to tell about yourself. The word* **I** *goes in the naming part of the sentence. The word* **me** *goes in the telling part. Find and circle* **I** *and* **me** *in these sentences.*

DAY 2

Read the rule aloud. Then guide students through the activities.

- **Activity A:** Say: *The words in the box are either naming parts or telling parts. Let's place them in the correct part of the chart.* Direct students to the first phrase and ask: *Is* **buy the treats** *a naming part or a telling part? Does it tell who is doing the action or what is being done?* (what is being done) Say: **Buy the treats** *is a telling part.* You may wish to have students work in pairs to complete the chart.

- **Activity B:** Say: *Now choose one of the naming parts. Write a complete sentence using that naming part and your own telling part.* Model if necessary.

- **Activity C:** Say: *Write a complete sentence using a telling part from the chart and your own naming part.* Model if necessary.

- **Activity D (Convention):** Say: *We use the words* **I** *and* **me** *in certain places. Complete each sentence with the correct word.*

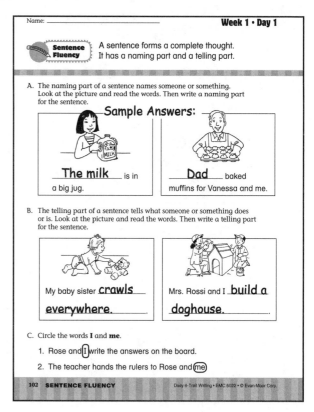

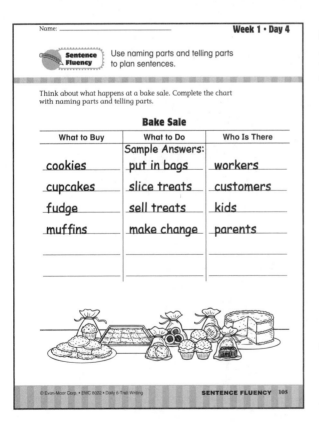

Name: _____ Week 1 • Day 3

Sentence Fluency — Write sentences with naming parts and telling parts.

A. Write four sentences about the picture. Circle the naming parts. Underline the telling parts.

Toys for Sale!

Sample Answers:

1. (A yo-yo) costs 75 cents. _____
2. (I) want to buy a monkey. _____
3. (The best toy) is the boat. _____
4. (Many toys) are for sale. _____

B. Finish the sentences about yourself and a friend. Put your friend's name first. Remember to use **I** and **me** correctly.

1. __Friend__ and __I__ went to the school fair.
2. Dad bought a toy for __Friend__ and __me__ .

104 SENTENCE FLUENCY   Daily 6-Trait Writing • EMC 6022 • © Evan-Moor Corp.

Name: _____ Week 1 • Day 4

Sentence Fluency — Use naming parts and telling parts to plan sentences.

Think about what happens at a bake sale. Complete the chart with naming parts and telling parts.

Bake Sale

What to Buy	What to Do	Who Is There
	Sample Answers:	
cookies	put in bags	workers
cupcakes	slice treats	customers
fudge	sell treats	kids
muffins	make change	parents

© Evan-Moor Corp. • EMC 6022 • Daily 6-Trait Writing   SENTENCE FLUENCY 105

DAY 3

Read the rule aloud. Then guide students through the activities.

- **Activity A:** Discuss the picture with students, identifying the setting and items. Then say: *Let's write complete sentences about this picture. Be sure to include a naming part and a telling part.* Model forming a sentence from the picture, if necessary. (e.g., Many toys are for sale.) After students write their sentences, say: *Look at the sentences you just wrote. Circle the naming part of each one. Then underline the telling part.* Circulate to check for skill acquisition and to offer assistance.

- **Activity B (Convention):** Say: *When you tell about someone else and yourself, always put yourself last. It's polite to mention someone else before yourself.* To illustrate, write this sentence on the board: *Mom drove Kelly and me to the fair.* Ask: *Which comes first, **Kelly** or **me**?* (**Kelly**) Then write: *Kelly and I found the toys.* Ask: *Which comes first, **Kelly** or **I**?* (**Kelly**) Have students complete the activity.

DAY 4

Read the rule aloud. Then guide students through the activity.

- Say: *This chart will help us plan our ideas. When you plan, or prewrite, you don't have to write complete sentences. It's more important to just put your ideas on paper.*

- Reproduce the chart on the board. Review the concept of bake sales. (e.g., what happens at them, who holds them, and why) Ask questions to prompt students' ideas and write their responses in the appropriate columns. Have students complete their charts independently or with a partner. Then say: *Now that we have our ideas, we can take them and write complete sentences.*

DAY 5 *Writing Prompt*

- *Describe a bake sale. Use the naming parts and telling parts you wrote on Day 4 to form sentences.*

- *Be sure to use the words **I** and **me** correctly.*

Sentence Fluency

A sentence forms a complete thought.
It has a naming part and a telling part.

A. The naming part of a sentence names someone or something.
Look at the picture and read the words. Then write a naming part
for the sentence.

_____ is in

a big jug.

_____ baked

muffins for Vanessa and me.

B. The telling part of a sentence tells what someone or something does
or is. Look at the picture and read the words. Then write a telling part
for the sentence.

My baby sister _____

_____.

Mrs. Rossi and I _____

_____.

C. Circle the words **I** and **me**.

1. Rose and I write the answers on the board.

2. The teacher hands the rulers to Rose and me.

Sentence Fluency Write sentences with naming parts and telling parts.

A. A sentence has a naming part and a telling part.
Read the sentence parts. Write them in the chart.

buy the treats	I	the bake sale
choose a brownie	cost 25 cents	will raise money
the cookies	people	

Naming Parts	Telling Parts

B. Use a naming part from the chart to write a complete sentence.

_____

C. Use a telling part from the chart to write a complete sentence.

_____

D. Write **I** or **me** to complete the sentences.

1. Grandpa pours milk for Rico and _____.

2. Rico and _____ drink the milk.

Sentence Fluency

Write sentences with naming parts and telling parts.

A. Write four sentences about the picture. Circle the naming parts. Underline the telling parts.

1. _____

2. _____

3. _____

4. _____

B. Finish the sentences about yourself and a friend. Put your friend's name first. Remember to use **I** and **me** correctly.

1. _____ and _____ went to the school fair.

2. Dad bought a toy for _____ and _____.

Sentence Fluency

Use naming parts and telling parts to plan sentences.

Think about what happens at a bake sale. Complete the chart with naming parts and telling parts.

Bake Sale

What to Buy	What to Do	Who Is There
_____	_____	_____
_____	_____	_____
_____	_____	_____
_____	_____	_____
_____	_____	_____
_____	_____	_____

SENTENCE FLUENCY
Write Longer Sentences

DAY 1

Read the rule aloud. Then say: *In good writing, we often find sentences of different lengths. Some are shorter and some are longer. By adding words to a sentence we not only make it longer, but also smoother and clearer.* Write the following sentences on the board: *1) Olivia saw a spider web. 2) This morning, Olivia saw a spider web in a bush.* Have a student underline the words that were added in sentence 2. Then ask: *Which sentence tells more clearly what happened?* (2—It tells when and where Olivia saw a spider web.) Guide students through the activities.

- **Activity A:** Read the first pair of sentences. Ask: *Which sentence is more clear? Why?* (2—It has more information; it asks a more specific question.) Have students find and underline the words that were added. Repeat for the remaining pairs.

- **Activity B (Convention):** Say: *When you list three or more things, use commas to separate the things.* Direct students to the last sentence in Activity A. Write it on the board and have students identify the three items listed. (**busy, strong, fun to watch**) Then point out the commas and have students find and circle the commas on their papers. Say: *The commas help us read with pauses so the words don't bump into each other.* Demonstrate by reading the sentence aloud with and without pauses.

DAY 2

Read the rule aloud. Then guide students through the activities.

- **Activity A:** Write these sentences on the board: *The little caterpillar munched on leaves. The little caterpillar munched on leaves without stopping.* Ask: *Which words tell **how** the little caterpillar munched?* (**without stopping**) Then say: *We can make sentences longer by adding words that tell **when**, **where**, or **how**. Those words can make our ideas clearer to the reader.* Have students complete the activity.

- **Activity B:** Say: *Now, let's add our own words to tell **when**, **where**, and **how**.* To prompt student ideas, ask questions such as: *Where do bees work? When do crickets usually chirp? Do butterflies make noise? When does the sun shine?*

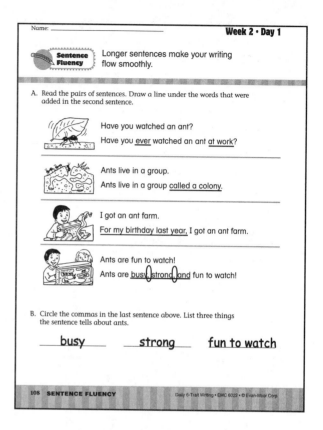

Name: _____ **Week 2 • Day 1**

Sentence Fluency — Longer sentences make your writing flow smoothly.

A. Read the pairs of sentences. Draw a line under the words that were added in the second sentence.

Have you watched an ant?
Have you <u>ever</u> watched an ant <u>at work</u>?

Ants live in a group.
Ants live in a group <u>called a colony</u>.

I got an ant farm.
<u>For my birthday last year,</u> I got an ant farm.

Ants are fun to watch!
Ants are <u>busy, strong, and</u> fun to watch!

B. Circle the commas in the last sentence above. List three things the sentence tells about ants.

<u>busy</u>   <u>strong</u>   <u>fun to watch</u>

Name: _____ **Week 2 • Day 2**

Sentence Fluency — Add words that tell **when**, **where**, and **how** to write longer sentences.

A. Read the sentences. Underline the words that tell **when**, **where**, or **how**.

1. (where) The bees were buzzing <u>in the roses</u>.

2. (when) <u>Every afternoon,</u> a lizard visits the garden.

3. (how) The cricket chirps <u>over and over</u>.

B. Read the sentences. Add words that tell **when**, **where**, or **how** to make the sentences longer. **Sample Answers:**

1. The bees are working. (where)
   <u>The bees are working in their hive.</u>

2. I heard a cricket chirp. (when)
   <u>I heard a cricket chirp last night.</u>

3. A butterfly flew away. (how)
   <u>A butterfly flew away quietly.</u>

4. The sun shines. (when)
   <u>The sun shines all day long.</u>

Week 2 · Day 3 worksheet

Name: _____

Week 2 · Day 3

Sentence Fluency — Use lists to write longer sentences.

A. Read the sentences. Add commas to the lists.

1. The beetle uses its mouth for cutting, biting, and chewing.

2. Grasshoppers, crickets, and some spiders are good jumpers.

3. Ants, bees, and wasps live in colonies.

4. Some butterflies are called skippers, blues, or coppers.

5. Caterpillars make cocoons, turn into butterflies, and fly away.

B. Write a sentence listing three insects you like or do not like. Use commas.

Sample Answers:

I like ladybugs, dragonflies, and lightning bugs.

C. Write a sentence telling three things that some insects do. Use commas.

Some insects fly, crawl, or buzz.

110 SENTENCE FLUENCY — Daily 6-Trait Writing • EMC 6022 • © Evan-Moor Corp.

DAY 3

Read the rule aloud. Then say: *Listing things or actions is another way to make your sentences longer.* Guide students through the activities.

- **Activity A (Convention):** Model adding commas to item 1. Write it on the board and ask: *What action words are listed in the sentence?* (**cutting**, **biting**, and **chewing**) Then say: *The commas go after the first two things in the list.* Write the commas in the sentence. You may wish to complete item 5 as a group.

- **Activity B:** Together, brainstorm a list of insects (e.g., moth, dragonfly, ladybug, mosquito, wasp) and write them on the board for reference. Have students choose three to use in their sentence.

- **Activity C:** Brainstorm a list of verbs that apply to insects (e.g., fly, buzz, sting, annoy, bite, crawl, flutter), and have students choose three to use in their sentence.

Week 2 · Day 4 worksheet

Name: _____

Week 2 · Day 4

Sentence Fluency — Write longer sentences.

Here are some sentences for a story. Write words and phrases that you might use to make the sentences longer.

Sample Answers:

June Bug had a picnic. (where)
1. by the lake
2. on the hill
3. in her yard

They sang. (how)
1. along with Cricket's fiddle
2. loudly
3. together

June Bug's Picnic

They danced. (when)
1. that evening
2. all night
3. until morning

Everyone ate. (what)
1. pie, watermelon, and salad
2. sandwiches, chips, and apples
3. bread, fruit, and water

© Evan-Moor Corp. • EMC 6022 • Daily 6-Trait Writing — SENTENCE FLUENCY 111

DAY 4

Read the rule aloud. Then guide students through the activity.

- Say: *Today, we are going to write our ideas for a story called "June Bug's Picnic." In this story, the insects are having a picnic, just like people would.* Point out that each box in the web has a short sentence and a phrase. Read the sentence and sample phrase in the first box. Then ask: *Where else could June Bug have a picnic?* (e.g., up in a tree, in her yard) Have students write their phrases in the box.

- Ask students to complete the remaining boxes by writing words or phrases that could be used to make each sentence longer and clearer. Point out that the words in parentheses give clues about what kind of phrases to write. You may wish to have students complete the web in pairs.

DAY 5 *Writing Prompt*

- *Write a story entitled "June Bug's Picnic." Use the sentences and words you wrote in the web on Day 4.*

- *Be sure to use commas to separate items in a list.*

Sentence Fluency — Longer sentences make your writing flow smoothly.

A. Read the pairs of sentences. Draw a line under the words that were added in the second sentence.

Have you watched an ant?

Have you ever watched an ant at work?

Ants live in a group.

Ants live in a group called a colony.

I got an ant farm.

For my birthday last year, I got an ant farm.

Ants are fun to watch!

Ants are busy, strong, and fun to watch!

B. Circle the commas in the last sentence above. List three things the sentence tells about ants.

_____   _____   _____

Sentence Fluency

Add words that tell **when**, **where**, and **how** to write longer sentences.

A. Read the sentences. Underline the words that tell **when**, **where**, or **how**.

1. (where) The bees were buzzing in the roses.

2. (when) Every afternoon, a lizard visits the garden.

3. (how) The cricket chirps over and over.

B. Read the sentences. Add words that tell **when**, **where**, or **how** to make the sentences longer.

1. The bees are working. (where)

_____

2. I heard a cricket chirp. (when)

_____

3. A butterfly flew away. (how)

_____

4. The sun shines. (when)

_____

Name: _____

 **Sentence Fluency**   Use lists to write longer sentences.

A. Read the sentences. Add commas to the lists.

1. The beetle uses its mouth for cutting biting and chewing.

2. Grasshoppers crickets and some spiders are good jumpers.

3. Ants bees and wasps live in colonies.

4. Some butterflies are called skippers blues or coppers.

5. Caterpillars make cocoons turn into butterflies and fly away.

B. Write a sentence listing three insects you like or do not like. Use commas.

_____

_____

C. Write a sentence telling three things that some insects do. Use commas.

_____

_____

   Daily 6-Trait Writing • EMC 6022 • © Evan-Moor Corp.

Sentence Fluency   Write longer sentences.

Here are some sentences for a story. Write words and phrases that you might use to make the sentences longer.

June Bug had a picnic. **(where)**

1. by the lake _____

2. _____

3. _____

They sang. **(how)**

1. along with Cricket's fiddle

2. _____

3. _____

June Bug's Picnic

They danced. **(when)**

1. that evening _____

2. _____

3. _____

Everyone ate. **(what)**

1. pie, watermelon, and salad _____

2. _____

3. _____

DAY 1

Say: *Although longer sentences are often an improvement, make sure you don't write run-on sentences. Run-on sentences are made up of two or more sentences that run together.* Write the following on the board: *The birds couldn't find a drop to drink, the crow was very thirsty luckily, he found a pitcher with water in it.* Point out that a run-on sentence can be confusing and difficult to read. Read the rule aloud. Then guide students through the activities.

- **Activity A:** Direct students to item 1. Ask: *Which of these is a run-on sentence?* (the first) *How do you know?* (no period; ideas run together) Then say: *Choice 2 is a compound sentence. It uses the same ideas from the first sentence, but combines them with a comma and the word **and**. That makes the sentence correct.* Repeat the comparison of sentences for items 2 through 4.

- **Activity B (Convention):** Say: *One way to fix a run-on sentence is to make it a compound sentence. A compound sentence is two sentences combined with a comma and a joining word, such as **and**. You can also divide the run-on into two separate sentences.* Have students complete the activity independently or as a group.

DAY 2

Read the rule aloud. Then say: *Rambling sentences have too many **ands** and **buts**.* Use the first sentence in Activity A as an example. Then say: *For sentences like these, we have to separate the ideas into smaller sentences.* Guide students through the activities.

- **Activity A:** Read the first sentence aloud and ask: *What are the different ideas in this sentence?* (drum and trumpet are loud; violin and piano are soft) Say: *That's a lot of ideas for one sentence! How can we separate them?* (divide into loud and soft instruments) Guide students in breaking the sentence into two or more new sentences. (e.g., A drum and a trumpet are loud, but a violin is soft. A piano is soft, too.) Review how to use proofreading marks and have students complete the activity.

- **Activity B:** After reading the directions aloud, point out that there may be multiple "right" answers. Have students complete the activity and then read aloud their new sentences.

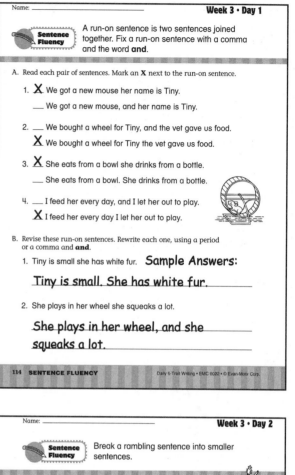

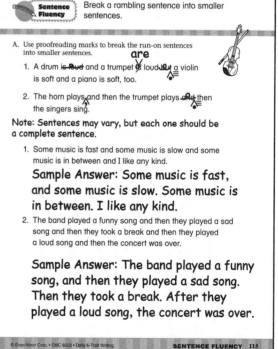

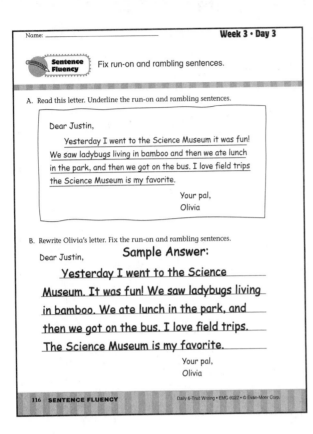

Sentence Fluency — Fix run-on and rambling sentences.

A. Read this letter. Underline the run-on and rambling sentences.

Dear Justin,

   Yesterday I went to the Science Museum it was fun! We saw ladybugs living in bamboo and then we ate lunch in the park, and then we got on the bus. I love field trips the Science Museum is my favorite.

Your pal,
Olivia

B. Rewrite Olivia's letter. Fix the run-on and rambling sentences.

Dear Justin,

Sample Answer:

Yesterday I went to the Science Museum. It was fun! We saw ladybugs living in bamboo. We ate lunch in the park, and then we got on the bus. I love field trips. The Science Museum is my favorite.

Your pal,
Olivia

116 SENTENCE FLUENCY   Daily 6-Trait Writing • EMC 6022 • © Evan-Moor Corp.

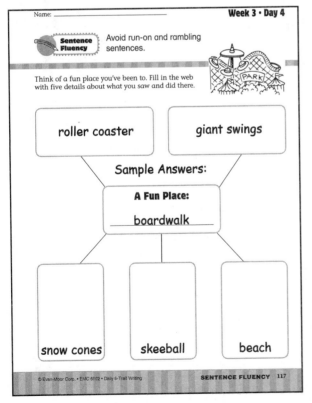

Sentence Fluency — Avoid run-on and rambling sentences.

Think of a fun place you've been to. Fill in the web with five details about what you saw and did there.

roller coaster   giant swings

Sample Answers:

A Fun Place:
boardwalk

snow cones   skeeball   beach

© Evan-Moor Corp. • EMC 6022 • Daily 6-Trait Writing   SENTENCE FLUENCY 117

DAY 3

Read the rule aloud. Say: *One way to learn not to use run-on or rambling sentences in your own writing is to look for them in others' writing. The more you notice how they make the text hard to read, the better you will get at avoiding them!* Then say: *One way to spot run-on and rambling sentences is to read aloud. This helps us hear the rhythm and flow of the words.* Guide students through the activities.

- **Activity A:** Instruct students to listen carefully and follow along as you read the letter aloud. Be sure to read it as written so students can "hear" the errors. After you read, go back through the letter one sentence at a time. Have students identify the run-on and rambling sentences.

- **Activity B:** Say: *Let's make Olivia's letter better!* Review how to fix run-on and rambling sentences. Have students complete the activity on their own or in small groups. Circulate to provide assistance. When finished, have students read aloud their edited paragraphs. Emphasize that there is more than one right answer.

DAY 4

Read the rule aloud. Then guide students through the activity.

- Say: *Let's plan a letter to a friend. We can write about a fun place we've visited.* Ask: *What are some fun places you've been to?* Record responses on the board.

- Have students choose a place to write about. Then say: *Write the name of the place in the center of your web. Then think of five details about that place. What did you see? What did you do?* Circulate to help students complete the web.

DAY 5 *Writing Prompt*

- *Write a letter to a friend telling about a fun place you've been to. Use the details you wrote on Day 4. Combine at least two details into one compound sentence.*

- *Be careful not to write run-on or rambling sentences. Remember, you can use a comma and the word **and**, or you can break a long sentence into two.*

Sentence Fluency

A run-on sentence is two sentences joined together. Fix a run-on sentence with a comma and the word **and**.

A. Read each pair of sentences. Mark an **X** next to the run-on sentence.

1. ___ We got a new mouse her name is Tiny.

   ___ We got a new mouse, and her name is Tiny.

2. ___ We bought a wheel for Tiny, and the vet gave us food.

   ___ We bought a wheel for Tiny the vet gave us food.

3. ___ She eats from a bowl she drinks from a bottle.

   ___ She eats from a bowl. She drinks from a bottle.

4. ___ I feed her every day, and I let her out to play.

   ___ I feed her every day I let her out to play.

B. Revise these run-on sentences. Rewrite each one, using a period or a comma and **and**.

1. Tiny is small she has white fur.

   _____

2. She plays in her wheel she squeaks a lot.

   _____

   _____

Daily 6-Trait Writing • EMC 6022 • © Evan-Moor Corp.

Sentence Fluency

Break a rambling sentence into smaller sentences.

A. Use proofreading marks to break the run-on sentences into smaller sentences.

1. A drum is loud and a trumpet is loud but a violin is soft and a piano is soft, too.

2. The horn plays and then the trumpet plays and then the singers sing.

B. Rewrite each run-on sentence. Turn it into two or more smaller sentences.

1. Some music is fast and some music is slow and some music is in between and I like any kind.

   _____

   _____

2. The band played a funny song and then they played a sad song and then they took a break and then they played a loud song and then the concert was over.

   _____

   _____

   _____

   _____

 **Sentence Fluency**   Fix run-on and rambling sentences.

A. Read this letter. Underline the run-on and rambling sentences.

> Dear Justin,
>
> Yesterday I went to the Science Museum it was fun! We saw ladybugs living in bamboo and then we ate lunch in the park, and then we got on the bus. I love field trips the Science Museum is my favorite.
>
> Your pal,
> Olivia

B. Rewrite Olivia's letter. Fix the run-on and rambling sentences.

Dear Justin,

_____

_____

_____

_____

_____

Your pal,
Olivia

    Daily 6-Trait Writing • EMC 6022 • © Evan-Moor Corp.

Sentence Fluency

Avoid run-on and rambling sentences.

Think of a fun place you've been to. Fill in the web with five details about what you saw and did there.

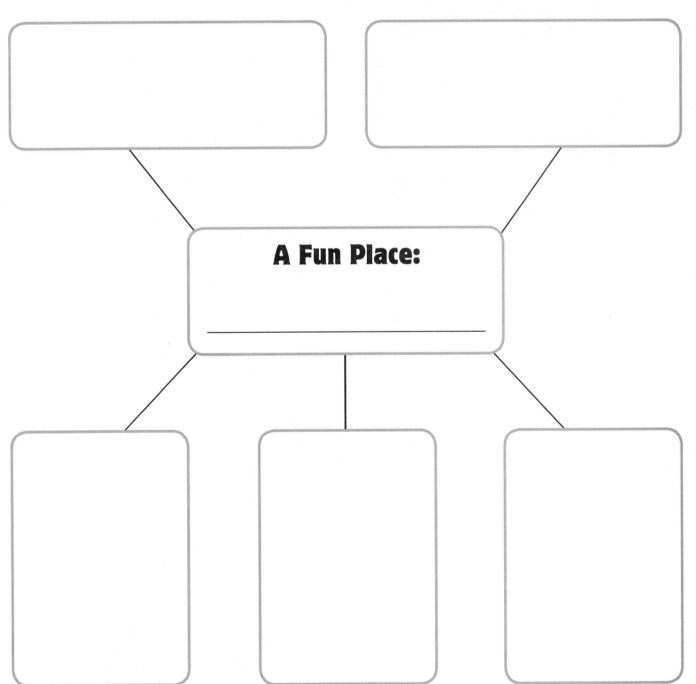

A Fun Place:

_____

SENTENCE FLUENCY
Combine Choppy Sentences

DAY 1

Read the rule aloud. Then say: *You know that good writers use short and long sentences. Too many short sentences in a row can sound choppy. Sometimes we can combine two short sentences into one longer one.* Guide students through the activities.

- **Activity A:** Write these examples on the board: *Frogs have four legs. Frogs have large eyes.* Ask: *How can we fix these choppy sentences?* (Combine them into one smoother sentence.) Ask for suggestions. (e.g., Frogs have four legs and large eyes.) Say: *By combining the sentences, we made our writing smoother.* Direct students to complete the activity. You may wish to do this as a group.

- **Activity B (Convention):** Say: *Another way to combine sentences is to form a compound sentence.* Review that a compound sentence is made up of two or more simple sentences joined by a comma and a joining word, such as **and**, **but**, or **or**. Write the following example on the board: *Tadpoles stay underwater, but frogs can go on land.* Circle the comma and the joining word **but**.

DAY 2

Read the rule aloud. Then guide students through the activity.

- Write the sentences in item 1 on the board. Say: *These sentences sound a little choppy. Let's combine them into one compound sentence.* Ask: *Which joining word should we use?* Review that **and** is used to mean "also" or "then," **but** is used to compare two things, and **or** shows a choice between two things. Guide students to recognize that **but** makes the most sense in this case because you are comparing what you saw and what you didn't see.

- Write the compound sentence on the board. Ask: *What is the joining word?* (**but**) *What comes just before the word* **but**? (a comma)

- Have students complete the activity. Circulate to check for correct construction of compound sentences. Then ask volunteers to read aloud their sentences. Say: *Listen how the compound sentences flow better and make the writing smoother.*

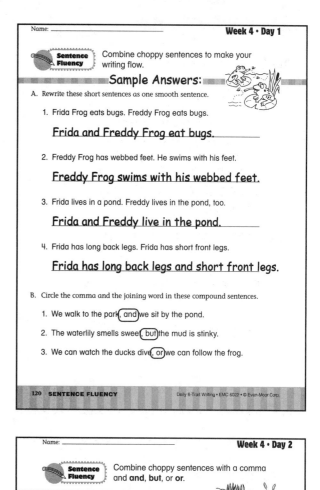

Name: _____   Week 4 • Day 1

Sentence Fluency — Combine choppy sentences to make your writing flow.

Sample Answers:

A. Rewrite these short sentences as one smooth sentence.

1. Frida Frog eats bugs. Freddy Frog eats bugs.

   Frida and Freddy Frog eat bugs.

2. Freddy Frog has webbed feet. He swims with his feet.

   Freddy Frog swims with his webbed feet.

3. Frida lives in a pond. Freddy lives in the pond, too.

   Frida and Freddy live in the pond.

4. Frida has long back legs. Frida has short front legs.

   Frida has long back legs and short front legs.

B. Circle the comma and the joining word in these compound sentences.

1. We walk to the park, and we sit by the pond.

2. The waterlily smells sweet, but the mud is stinky.

3. We can watch the ducks dive, or we can follow the frog.

120 SENTENCE FLUENCY   Daily 6-Trait Writing • EMC 6022 • © Evan-Moor Corp.

Name: _____   Week 4 • Day 2

Sentence Fluency — Combine choppy sentences with a comma and **and**, **but**, or **or**.

Combine the sentences into compound sentences.

Sample Answers:

1. We saw a fish. We didn't see a turtle.

   We saw a fish, but we didn't see a turtle.

2. We can wade in the water. We can eat lunch.

   We can wade in the water, or we can eat lunch.

3. I like to play in the mud. I like to count the ducks.

   I like to play in the mud, and I like to count the ducks.

4. Baby geese stay with their parents. Baby turtles leave.

   Baby geese stay with their parents, but baby turtles leave.

5. A dragonfly begins its life underwater. It ends its life in the air.

   A dragonfly begins its life underwater, and/but ends its life in the air.

© Evan-Moor Corp. • EMC 6022 • Daily 6-Trait Writing   SENTENCE FLUENCY 121

Worksheet: Week 4 · Day 3

Name: _____ Week 4 · Day 3

Sentence Fluency Combine choppy sentences.

Read the paragraph. Underline the choppy sentences. Combine them to write new sentences on the lines.

The Life Cycle of a Moth

All moths change as they grow. A caterpillar hatches from an egg. <u>It eats. It grows.</u> Then the caterpillar spins a cocoon around its body. <u>The caterpillar changes. It changes into an adult.</u> The adult moth climbs out of the cocoon. <u>Its wings dry. It flies away.</u>

Sample Answers:

1. It eats and grows.

2. The caterpillar changes into an adult.

3. Its wings dry, and it flies away.

122 SENTENCE FLUENCY   Daily 6-Trait Writing • EMC 6022 • © Evan-Moor Corp.

Worksheet: Week 4 · Day 4

Name: _____ Week 4 · Day 4

Sentence Fluency Make your writing flow.

Write short sentences or phrases to describe each stage in the life cycle of a frog.

The Life Cycle of a Frog

Sample Answers:

- eggs are laid
- egg becomes tadpole
- grows 2 legs
- has 4 legs and a short tail
- becomes adult frog

© Evan-Moor Corp. • EMC 6022 • Daily 6-Trait Writing   SENTENCE FLUENCY 123

DAY 3

Read the rule aloud. Then say: *We have learned that good writers use sentences of different lengths. Too many short sentences in a row can be choppy. To make them smoother, we can combine them. But there's more than one way to do this, so look for the best way.*

Write the following sentences on the board: *Our class went on a field trip. We went to a pond.* Then write the following combined sentences: *1) Our class went on a field trip, and we went to a pond. 2) Our class went on a field trip to a pond.* Ask: *Which is better?* (The second one, because it's smoother and less wordy.) Then guide students through the activity.

- Before reading, say: *As we read this paragraph, listen for choppy sentences. Underline the sentences you think should be combined.* Then read the paragraph aloud.

- Say: *Look back at the sentences you underlined. How can you combine them? Which way sounds best? Write the new sentences on the lines.* You may want to have students complete this activity in pairs. Then have them share their combined sentences.

DAY 4

Read the rule aloud. Then guide students through the activity.

- Say: *For our writing prompt this week, we will describe the life cycle of a frog.* Using the pictures, review the life cycle and answer any questions students may have.

- Have students write key words, phrases, or sentences for each picture. You may wish to model combining phrases into sentences using the key words. (e.g., tail then legs—At first, a tadpole has only a tail, but then it grows two legs.)

DAY 5 *Writing Prompt*

- *Describe the life cycle of a frog. Combine the sentences and phrases you wrote on Day 4. Use at least one compound sentence.*

- *Be sure to form compound sentences correctly with a comma and a joining word.*

Sentence Fluency

Combine choppy sentences to make your writing flow.

A. Rewrite these short sentences as one smooth sentence.

1. Frida Frog eats bugs. Freddy Frog eats bugs.

   _____

2. Freddy Frog has webbed feet. He swims with his feet.

   _____

3. Frida lives in a pond. Freddy lives in the pond, too.

   _____

4. Frida has long back legs. Frida has short front legs.

   _____

B. Circle the comma and the joining word in these compound sentences.

1. We walk to the park, and we sit by the pond.

2. The waterlily smells sweet, but the mud is stinky.

3. We can watch the ducks dive, or we can follow the frog.

   Daily 6-Trait Writing • EMC 6022 • © Evan-Moor Corp.

Sentence Fluency

Combine choppy sentences with a comma and **and**, **but**, or **or**.

Combine the sentences into compound sentences.

1. We saw a fish. We didn't see a turtle.

   _____

2. We can wade in the water. We can eat lunch.

   _____

3. I like to play in the mud. I like to count the ducks.

   _____

   _____

4. Baby geese stay with their parents. Baby turtles leave.

   _____

   _____

5. A dragonfly begins its life underwater. It ends its life in the air.

   _____

   _____

Sentence Fluency   Combine choppy sentences.

Read the paragraph. Underline the choppy sentences. Combine them to write new sentences on the lines.

The Life Cycle of a Moth

All moths change as they grow. A caterpillar hatches from an egg. It eats. It grows. Then the caterpillar spins a cocoon around its body. The caterpillar changes. It changes into an adult. The adult moth climbs out of the cocoon. Its wings dry. It flies away.

1. _____

_____

2. _____

_____

3. _____

_____

Sentence Fluency

Make your writing flow.

Write short sentences or phrases to describe each stage in the life cycle of a frog.

The Life Cycle of a Frog

Read the rule aloud. Then review: *The naming part names someone or something. The telling part tells what someone or something does or is.* Write the following sentence on the board and have students identify the parts: *A hummingbird's wings make a humming sound.* (naming: "A hummingbird's wings"; telling: "make a humming sound") Then guide students through the activities.

- **Activity A:** Read the directions and sentence 1. Ask: *Which part of the sentence names someone or something? Circle it. Which part tells what the spider monkeys do? Underline it.* Have students complete the activity independently.

- **Activity B:** Read the naming parts. Then ask: *What could each of these animals do? Write a telling part that says what the animal does.* You may wish to brainstorm ideas as a group.

- **Activity C (Convention):** Say: *We add **er** to an adjective to compare two people, places, or things. We add **est** to an adjective to compare three or more people, places, or things.* Read sentence 1 aloud. Ask: *Which word compares how fast two things are?* (**faster**) *Which word compares how slow three or more animals are?* (**slowest**) Say: *The three-toed sloth is the slowest of all the mammals in the rainforest.*

Read the rule aloud. Then review: *To make sentences longer, use words that tell **when**, **where**, and **how**.* Write this sentence on the board: *We took a walk in the rainforest.* Ask: *Which words answer the question **where**?* ("in the rainforest") Say: *The words not only make the sentence longer, but also clearer.* Then guide students through the activities.

- **Activity A:** Read the phrases in the word box aloud. For sentence 1, ask: *Which phrase in the word box tells **when**?* Repeat for sentences 2 and 3.

- **Activity B:** Remind students: *You can write lists to make sentences longer.* Then review the use of commas to separate a list of three or more things. Have students complete the activity.

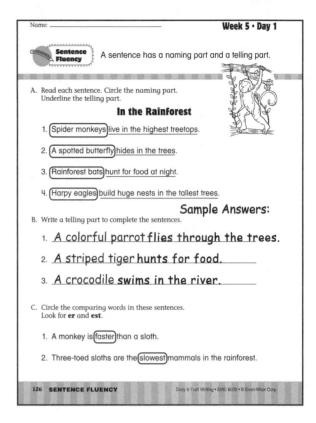

Name: _____ Week 5 • Day 1

Sentence Fluency A sentence has a naming part and a telling part.

A. Read each sentence. Circle the naming part. Underline the telling part.

In the Rainforest

1. Spider monkeys live in the highest treetops.
2. A spotted butterfly hides in the trees.
3. Rainforest bats hunt for food at night.
4. Harpy eagles build huge nests in the tallest trees.

Sample Answers:

B. Write a telling part to complete the sentences.

1. A colorful parrot flies through the trees.
2. A striped tiger hunts for food.
3. A crocodile swims in the river.

C. Circle the comparing words in these sentences. Look for **er** and **est**.

1. A monkey is faster than a sloth.
2. Three-toed sloths are the slowest mammals in the rainforest.

126 **SENTENCE FLUENCY** Daily 6-Trait Writing • EMC 6022 • © Evan-Moor Corp.

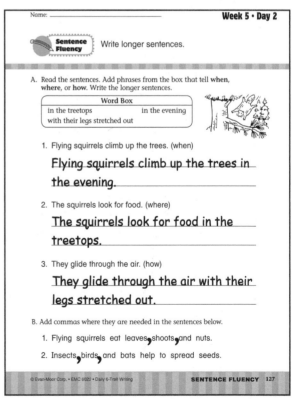

Name: _____ Week 5 • Day 2

Sentence Fluency Write longer sentences.

A. Read the sentences. Add phrases from the box that tell **when**, **where**, or **how**. Write the longer sentences.

Word Box	
in the treetops	in the evening
with their legs stretched out	

1. Flying squirrels climb up the trees. (when)

   Flying squirrels climb up the trees in the evening.

2. The squirrels look for food. (where)

   The squirrels look for food in the treetops.

3. They glide through the air. (how)

   They glide through the air with their legs stretched out.

B. Add commas where they are needed in the sentences below.

1. Flying squirrels eat leaves, shoots, and nuts.
2. Insects, birds, and bats help to spread seeds.

© Evan-Moor Corp. • EMC 6022 • Daily 6-Trait Writing **SENTENCE FLUENCY** 127

Name: _____ Week 5 • Day 3

Sentence Fluency Fix run-on and choppy sentences.

A. Read the paragraph aloud.

Life in the Rainforest

My family lives in a small village and it is in the rainforest and our house is near a river. The house is round many families live in it together. We work together, too. We grow crops. We hunt.

Sample Answer:

B. Fix the run-on and choppy sentences. Rewrite the paragraph.

My family lives in a small village. It is in the rainforest. Our house is near a river. The house is round, and many families live in it together. We work together, too. We grow crops, and we hunt.

C. Complete each sentence with a comparing word. Use **er** or **est**.

1. A cobra is __longer__ than a viper.
   (long)

2. The kapok tree is the __tallest__ tree in the rainforest.
   (tall)

128 **SENTENCE FLUENCY** Daily 6-Trait Writing • EMC 6022 • © Evan-Moor Corp.

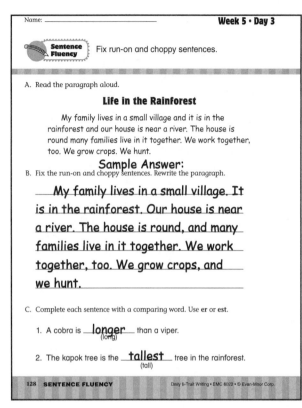

Name: _____ Week 5 • Day 4

Sentence Fluency Make your writing flow.

Pretend you went to the rainforest. Write short sentences or phrases to describe your adventure. **Sample Answers:**

Why I was there:
to see the
animals

How I felt:
excited
happy
scared

My Rainforest Adventure

What I saw:
monkeys
snakes
parrots
pretty flowers
waterfall

What happened:
ran from a snake,
splashed by the
waterfall

© Evan-Moor Corp. • EMC 6022 • Daily 6-Trait Writing **SENTENCE FLUENCY** 129

DAY 3

Read the rule aloud. Remind students that a run-on sentence is made up of two or more sentences that run together. Also review that too many short sentences in a row can sound choppy. If necessary, remind students how to construct compound sentences. Then guide them through the activities.

- **Activity A:** Read the paragraph aloud. Have students identify the run-on, rambling, and choppy sentences.

- **Activity B:** Remind students that there is more than one correct way to fix the paragraph. Circulate to provide assistance. Then have volunteers read their revised paragraphs aloud.

- **Activity C (Convention):** For each sentence, ask: *How many are being compared? Does the comparing word need* **er** *or* **est***?*

DAY 4

Read the rule aloud. Say: *We will use everything we've learned about sentences to make our writing flow. However, we must first plan what we will write.* Then guide students through the activity.

- Read the directions aloud. Have students discuss what they know about the rainforest. Help them brainstorm reasons why they might go there and what it would be like.

- Circulate to help students complete the web. Encourage them to include **where**, **when**, and **how** phrases to extend their sentences.

DAY 5 *Writing Prompt*

- *Use the ideas from Day 4 to write about your rainforest adventure! Try not to use run-ons or choppy sentences.*

- *Use at least one comparing word with* **er** *or* **est***.*

Sentence Fluency

A sentence has a naming part and a telling part.

A. Read each sentence. Circle the naming part. Underline the telling part.

In the Rainforest

1. Spider monkeys live in the highest treetops.

2. A spotted butterfly hides in the trees.

3. Rainforest bats hunt for food at night.

4. Harpy eagles build huge nests in the tallest trees.

B. Write a telling part to complete the sentences.

1. _A colorful parrot_ _____

2. _A striped tiger_ _____

3. _A crocodile_ _____

C. Circle the comparing words in these sentences. Look for **er** and **est**.

1. A monkey is faster than a sloth.

2. Three-toed sloths are the slowest mammals in the rainforest.

Sentence Fluency Write longer sentences.

A. Read the sentences. Add phrases from the box that tell **when**, **where**, or **how**. Write the longer sentences.

> **Word Box**
>
> in the treetops   in the evening
> with their legs stretched out

1. Flying squirrels climb up the trees. (when)

   _____

   _____

2. The squirrels look for food. (where)

   _____

   _____

3. They glide through the air. (how)

   _____

   _____

B. Add commas where they are needed in the sentences below.

   1. Flying squirrels eat leaves shoots and nuts.

   2. Insects birds and bats help to spread seeds.

Sentence Fluency   Fix run-on and choppy sentences.

A. Read the paragraph aloud.

Life in the Rainforest

My family lives in a small village and it is in the rainforest and our house is near a river. The house is round many families live in it together. We work together, too. We grow crops. We hunt.

B. Fix the run-on and choppy sentences. Rewrite the paragraph.

_____

_____

_____

_____

_____

_____

C. Complete each sentence with a comparing word. Use **er** or **est**.

1. A cobra is _____ than a viper.
              (long)

2. The kapok tree is the _____ tree in the rainforest.
                          (tall)

Name: _____

Sentence Fluency

Make your writing flow.

Pretend you went to the rainforest. Write short sentences or phrases to describe your adventure.

Why I was there:

_____

_____

_____

How I felt:

_____

_____

_____

My Rainforest Adventure

What I saw:

_____

_____

_____

What happened:

_____

_____

_____

VOICE
Use Formal and Informal Language

Refer to pages 6 and 7 to introduce or review the writing trait.

DAY 1

Write the words **formal** and **informal** on the board. Then say: *The kind of language we use in our writing changes when our purpose and our readers change. In a letter to the principal, you would use **formal** language. Formal language is the proper way to speak and write. You are careful to follow all the rules. In a note to your friend, you would use **informal** language. Informal language is the way we speak with friends and family. It sounds more relaxed and familiar.* Then guide students to complete the activities.

- **Activity A:** Read aloud the letter and e-mail. Then help students compare them by saying: *Look at the greetings.* (**Dear, Hi**) *Which is more formal?* (**Dear**) Continue pointing out differences, such as **thank you** versus **thanks**; **Your student** versus **xoxo**; and the use of abbreviations. Then have students answer the questions.

- **Activity B (Convention):** Say: *The words **was** and **were** tell about something that happened in the past. Use **was** to tell about one person or thing. Use **were** to tell about more than one person or thing. Also use **were** with the word **you**.* Help students find **was** and **were** in the letter and write the preceding word.

DAY 2

Read the rule aloud and review the meaning of formal language. Then write the following sentences on the board: *1) A family vacation at the Grand Canyon is exciting. 2) Our trip to the Grand Canyon was awesome!* Ask: *Which sentence would you use if you were writing a report?* (1) *Why?* (sounds more formal)

- **Activity A:** Read the report aloud. Ask: *What makes the language sound formal?* (phrases such as "There were many...," "You might wonder...," and "It is because...")

- **Activity B:** After reading each sentence, ask: *Is this formal or informal language? Should it be added to Drew's report? Why?*

- **Activity C (Convention):** Review the rules for using **was** and **were**. Then have students complete the sentences independently.

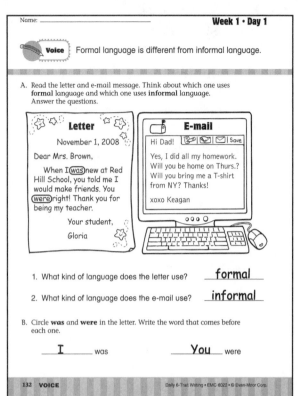

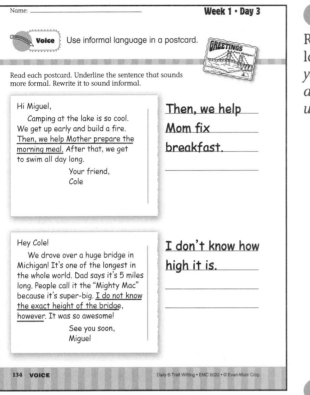

Name: _____ Week 1 • Day 3

Voice Use informal language in a postcard. GREETINGS from Michigan

Read each postcard. Underline the sentence that sounds more formal. Rewrite it to sound informal.

Hi Miguel,
    Camping at the lake is so cool. We get up early and build a fire. Then, we help Mother prepare the morning meal. After that, we get to swim all day long.
                Your friend,
                Cole

Then, we help
Mom fix
breakfast.
_____

Hey Cole!
    We drove over a huge bridge in Michigan! It's one of the longest in the whole world. Dad says it's 5 miles long. People call it the "Mighty Mac" because it's super-big. I do not know the exact height of the bridge, however. It was so awesome!
                See you soon,
                Miguel

I don't know how
high it is.
_____
_____

134 VOICE   Daily 6-Trait Writing • EMC 6022 • © Evan-Moor Corp.

DAY 3

Read the rule and review the meaning of informal language. Then say: *Even when using informal language, you need to explain your ideas, organize your writing, and stick to your topic. Otherwise, your readers may not understand you.* Guide students through the activities.

- Read the first postcard. Have students identify the sentence that uses formal language. ("Then, we help Mother prepare...") Ask: *Does this sentence fit with the rest of the postcard?* (no) Ask students to think of more informal words for **Mother**, **prepare**, and **morning meal**. (e.g., **Mom, make, breakfast**)

- Then read the second postcard. Have students identify the sentence that uses formal language. ("I do not know...") Ask: *Why doesn't this sentence fit with the other sentences?* (The words **do not know** and **exact height** sound like an adult.)

DAY 4

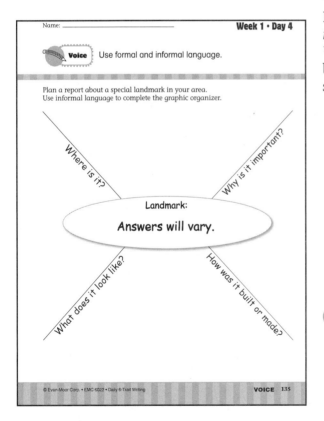

Name: _____ Week 1 • Day 4

Voice Use formal and informal language.

Plan a report about a special landmark in your area. Use informal language to complete the graphic organizer.

Where is it?

Why is it important?

Landmark:
Answers will vary.

What does it look like?

How was it built or made?

© Evan-Moor Corp. • EMC 6022 • Daily 6-Trait Writing   VOICE 135

Read the rule aloud. Say: *Whether we use formal or informal language depends on our purpose and audience. Which should we use in a graphic organizer?* (informal, because the audience is only yourself) Then guide students through the activity.

- If necessary, explain the meaning of **landmark**. Brainstorm different landmarks in your area. (e.g., buildings, monuments, natural attractions) Decide as a class which one to write about.

- As a class, list everything you know about the landmark. You may want to have students conduct further research to answer the questions in the graphic organizer. Then guide students in writing informal answers to the questions.

DAY 5 *Writing Prompt*

- *Write a report about a landmark in your area. Use formal language and the information you found on Day 4.*

- *Be sure to use **was** and **were** correctly.*

 **Voice** Formal language is different from informal language.

A. Read the letter and e-mail message. Think about which one uses **formal** language and which one uses **informal** language. Answer the questions.

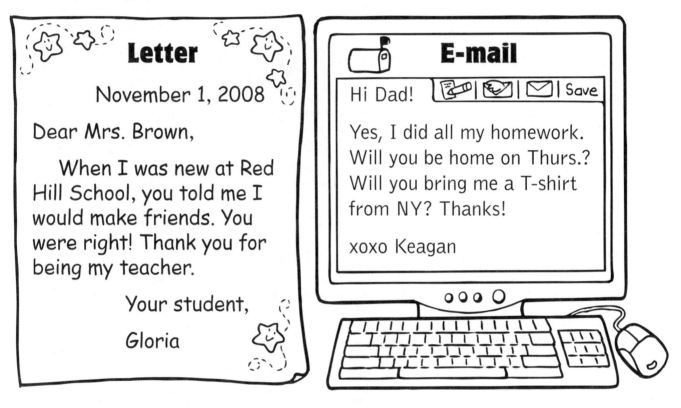

Letter

November 1, 2008

Dear Mrs. Brown,

When I was new at Red Hill School, you told me I would make friends. You were right! Thank you for being my teacher.

Your student,

Gloria

E-mail

Hi Dad! | Save

Yes, I did all my homework. Will you be home on Thurs.? Will you bring me a T-shirt from NY? Thanks!

xoxo Keagan

1. What kind of language does the letter use? _____

2. What kind of language does the e-mail use? _____

B. Circle **was** and **were** in the letter. Write the word that comes before each one.

_____ was   _____ were

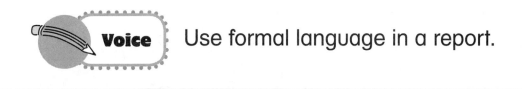

Use formal language in a report.

A. Read what Drew wrote in his report about a covered bridge.

A Bridge in the Country

Last fall, our family drove to the country. There were many colorful trees. Their leaves were red, orange, and gold. We also went to see White's Bridge. This is an old covered bridge. You might wonder why a bridge has a roof. It is because the bridge is made of wood, and wood rots if it gets wet. The roof is there to keep the wood dry.

B. Help Drew finish his report. Choose two sentences from below that use formal language. Write them on the lines.

The roof must have worked.   Check it out sometime.

The bridge is over 100 years old!   It was very cool.

_____

_____

C. Write **was** or **were** to complete each sentence.

1. We _____ in the country.

2. The trip _____ fun.

3. I'm glad you _____ there.

 **Voice** Use informal language in a postcard.

Read each postcard. Underline the sentence that sounds more formal. Rewrite it to sound informal.

Hi Miguel,

Camping at the lake is so cool. We get up early and build a fire. Then, we help Mother prepare the morning meal. After that, we get to swim all day long.

Your friend,
Cole

_____

_____

_____

_____

Hey Cole!

We drove over a huge bridge in Michigan! It's one of the longest in the whole world. Dad says it's 5 miles long. People call it the "Mighty Mac" because it's super-big. I do not know the exact height of the bridge, however. It was so awesome!

See you soon,
Miguel

_____

_____

_____

_____

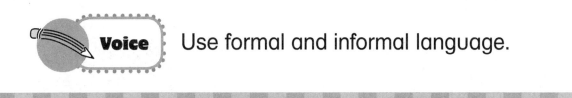

Voice Use formal and informal language.

Plan a report about a special landmark in your area.
Use informal language to complete the graphic organizer.

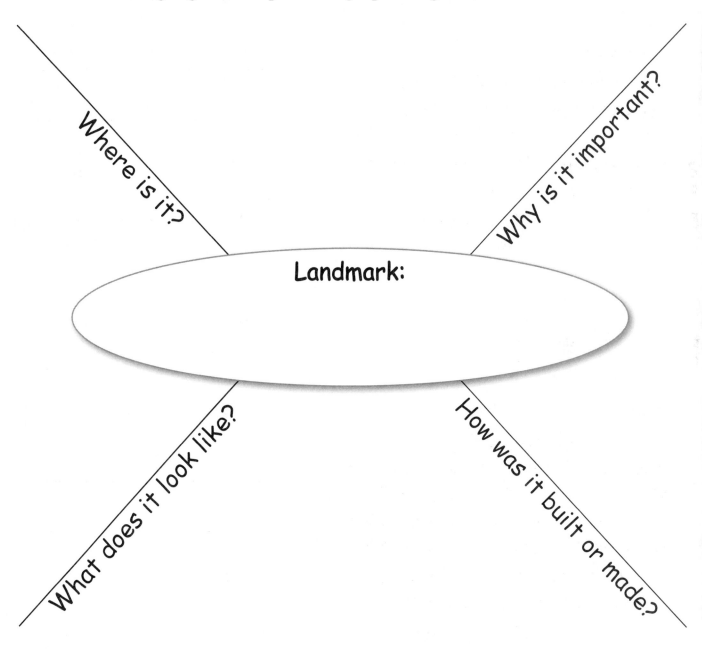

Where is it?

Why is it important?

Landmark:

What does it look like?

How was it built or made?

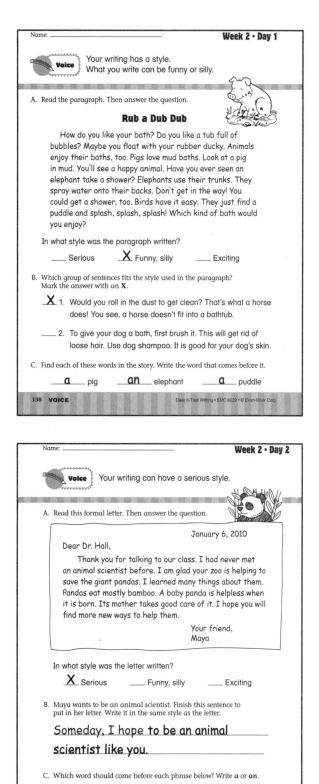

DAY 1

Read the rule aloud. Then say: *You already know that writers change their language to fit the purpose of their writing. Good writers also think about their **audience**, or who will read their writing.* Then guide students through the activities.

- **Activity A:** Read the paragraph aloud, emphasizing the humorous tone. Then ask: *In what style was the paragraph written?* (funny, silly) *How do you know?* Guide students to understand that the topic (animals take baths like people), word choice ("tub full of bubbles," "splash, splash, splash!"), and silly voice ("Don't get in the way!") all contribute to the style.

- **Activity B:** Ask: *What style should we look for in the sentences? What fits the paragraph?* (funny, silly) Read the sentences aloud, and discuss how their styles differ. (one is silly; one is more serious)

- **Activity C (Convention):** Review the difference between consonant sounds and vowel sounds, if necessary. Then say: *Use **a** before words that begin with a consonant sound. Use **an** before words that begin with a vowel sound.* Have students read each word and tell if it begins with a consonant or vowel sound before identifying the proper article.

DAY 2

Read the rule aloud. Then say: *Suppose we were writing a thank-you letter to a police officer who taught us about traffic safety. What style would we use—serious, funny, or exciting?* (serious) *Why?* (because staying safe is a serious topic) Guide students through the activities.

- **Activity A:** Ask: *What is the purpose of Maya's letter?* (to thank the scientist) *Who is the audience?* (Dr. Hall) *What is the style of the letter?* (serious)

- **Activity B:** Ask: *If you were Maya and wanted to be an animal scientist, how would you finish this sentence? Remember to keep it in a serious style.*

- **Activity C (Convention):** Review the use of **a** and **an**. Then read the phrases aloud, emphasizing the initial consonant sound in the first phrase and the vowel sound in the second phrase. Have students complete the activity independently.

Week 2 • Day 3

Name: _____

Voice Your writing can have an exciting style.

A. Owen wrote a book report in an exciting style. He wants to get others to read the book. Read the report and listen for Owen's voice.

Book Report

Name: Owen
Book Title: Hungry, Hungry Sharks!
Author: Joanna Cole

If you like sharks, this book is for you! Hungry, Hungry Sharks! is a nonfiction book. The facts I read made my mouth drop open. There are more than 300 kinds of sharks! Some are as small as your hand. Others are as long as a bus! Sharks use up thousands of teeth every year. This is because they eat so much. Most sharks eat fish, but some eat little shrimp or giant whales. Some have even eaten bottles, drums, and cans! I never knew sharks ate so many things. They really are very hungry!

B. Draw a line under two sentences that might make the reader excited about the book. **Answers will vary.**

C. Think about an exciting book you have read. Write two sentences that show your excitement about the book. Use **a** or **an** correctly.

1. _____**Answers will vary.**_____

_____

2. _____

140 VOICE   Daily 6-Trait Writing • EMC 6022 • © Evan-Moor Corp.

Week 2 • Day 4

Name: _____

Voice Write in a funny, serious, or exciting style.

Think of an interesting animal. What makes it interesting? Write your ideas in the web.

Purpose: to give information about _____

Audience: other students

Style: **funny, serious**, or exciting

Sample Answers:

- communicate by sound
- mammals
- Animal: dolphins
- flat tails
- curved dorsal fins

© Evan-Moor Corp. • EMC 6022 • Daily 6-Trait Writing   VOICE 141

DAY 3

Read the rule aloud. Then guide students through the activities.

- **Activity A:** Read the book report together. Then discuss Owen's use of adjectives, exclamation points, and feeling words. For example, ask: *What kind of punctuation mark ends the first sentence?* (exclamation point) *How do we know Owen was feeling amazed?* (his mouth "dropped open") *Name one amazing fact Owen included.* (e.g., "more than 300 kinds of sharks") *What exciting adjectives did Owen use?* (e.g., hungry, long, thousands, giant) Then have students tell whether Owen's exciting writing style made them want to read the book.

- **Activity B:** Have students read the sentences they underlined and tell what made those sentences exciting.

- **Activity C:** Brainstorm with students exciting books they have read. Ask: *What made those books exciting? What could you tell others about the book to convince them to read it? Use adjectives and feeling words to show your excitement.*

DAY 4

Read the rule aloud. Then guide students through the activity. Say: *Today, we're going to plan to write about an interesting animal. Our purpose is to give information about the animal. We'll be writing this for other students to read. You get to choose the animal and the style. Do you want to write in a funny, serious, or exciting style?*

After students choose their style, guide them to complete the web. Circulate among students to prompt ideas. For example, ask: *What animals have you read about recently? What have you studied in class?* Encourage students to write details about the animal that support the style they chose.

DAY 5 *Writing Prompt*

- *Use your web from Day 4 to write about an interesting animal. Choose a writing style that is funny, serious, or exciting.*

- *Be sure to use **a** and **an** correctly.*

Voice Your writing has a style.
What you write can be funny or silly.

A. Read the paragraph. Then answer the question.

Rub a Dub Dub

How do you like your bath? Do you like a tub full of
bubbles? Maybe you float with your rubber ducky. Animals
enjoy their baths, too. Pigs love mud baths. Look at a pig
in mud. You'll see a happy animal. Have you ever seen an
elephant take a shower? Elephants use their trunks. They
spray water onto their backs. Don't get in the way! You
could get a shower, too. Birds have it easy. They just find a
puddle and splash, splash, splash! Which kind of bath would
you enjoy?

In what style was the paragraph written?

_____ Serious   _____ Funny, silly   _____ Exciting

B. Which group of sentences fits the style used in the paragraph?
Mark the answer with an **X**.

_____ 1. Would you roll in the dust to get clean? That's what a horse
does! You see, a horse doesn't fit into a bathtub.

_____ 2. To give your dog a bath, first brush it. This will get rid of
loose hair. Use dog shampoo. It is good for your dog's skin.

C. Find each of these words in the story. Write the word that comes before it.

_____ pig   _____ elephant   _____ puddle

 **Voice** Your writing can have a serious style.

A. Read this formal letter. Then answer the question.

> January 6, 2010
>
> Dear Dr. Hall,
>
>   Thank you for talking to our class. I had never met an animal scientist before. I am glad your zoo is helping to save the giant pandas. I learned many things about them. Pandas eat mostly bamboo. A baby panda is helpless when it is born. Its mother takes good care of it. I hope you will find more new ways to help them.
>
>   Your friend,
>   Maya

In what style was the letter written?

_____ Serious _____ Funny, silly _____ Exciting

B. Maya wants to be an animal scientist. Finish this sentence to put in her letter. Write it in the same style as the letter.

Someday, I hope _____

_____

C. Which word should come before each phrase below? Write **a** or **an**.

_____ mother bear _____ angry baby

 **Voice** Your writing can have an exciting style.

A. Owen wrote a book report in an exciting style. He wants to get others to read the book. Read the report and listen for Owen's voice.

Book Report

Name: Owen
Book Title: <u>Hungry, Hungry Sharks!</u>
Author: Joanna Cole

If you like sharks, this book is for you! <u>Hungry, Hungry Sharks!</u> is a nonfiction book. The facts I read made my mouth drop open. There are more than 300 kinds of sharks! Some are as small as your hand. Others are as long as a bus! Sharks use up thousands of teeth every year. This is because they eat so much. Most sharks eat fish, but some eat little shrimp or giant whales. Some have even eaten bottles, drums, and cans! I never knew sharks ate so many things. They really are very hungry!

B. Draw a line under two sentences that might make the reader excited about the book.

C. Think about an exciting book you have read. Write two sentences that show your excitement about the book. Use **a** or **an** correctly.

1. _____

_____

2. _____

_____

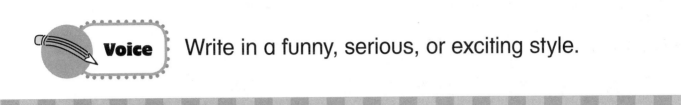

Voice Write in a funny, serious, or exciting style.

Think of an interesting animal. What makes it interesting?
Write your ideas in the web.

Purpose: to give information about _____

Audience: other students

Style: _____

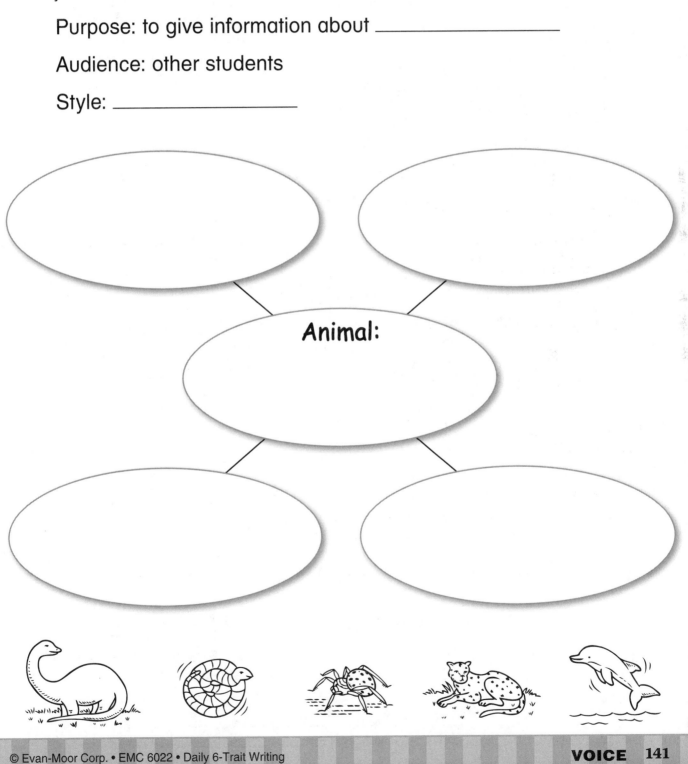

Animal:

DAY 1

Read the rule aloud. Ask: *Have you ever read a book that made you feel a certain way? Maybe it made you happy or sad. That feeling was the* **mood** *the author created. Writers use words to create happy, sad, scary, and even magical moods.* Then guide students through the activities.

- **Activity A:** Refer students to the first picture. Ask: *How does the picture make you feel?* (e.g., relaxed, peaceful, sleepy) *Why?* (shows a boy sleeping) Then read the sentence. Ask: *How does the sentence make you feel?* (the same) Ask: *What is the mood of the picture and sentence—angry or peaceful?* (peaceful) *What words does the writer use to create the mood?* (**quietly sleeping**) Repeat for the second picture.

- **Activity B:** After students have drawn their own pictures, have volunteers share what they drew and explain how they created a happy mood.

- **Activity C (Convention):** Say: *Spelling action words with* **ing** *can be tricky.* Have students find and write the word **sleeping** from Activity A. Say: *For this word, we simply add* **ing** *to the word* **sleep**. Then have students find and write **sitting**. Say: *For this word, we have to double the final consonant* **t** *before we add* **ing**. Have students circle the double **tt** in **sitting**.

DAY 2

Read the rule aloud. Say: *The words you use are important when creating a mood. They must match the mood of your story.* Ask: *What kinds of words might you use to create a magical mood?* (e.g., **dragon, princess, unicorn**) Write students' ideas on the board. Then guide them through the activities.

- **Activity A:** Read the example aloud. Ask: *Do robots create a magical mood? No! But kings and queens do, because they are often found in magical stories.* Then read item 1 and the words in the box aloud. Ask: *Which words in the word box could finish the sentence? Which would you see in a magical castle?* Have students complete the activity.

- **Activity B:** Ask: *What are some things that might happen in a castle?* Write students' ideas on the board. Then ask: *What describing words would help create a magical mood?* (e.g., sparkly, spooky, misty) Have students share their sentences.

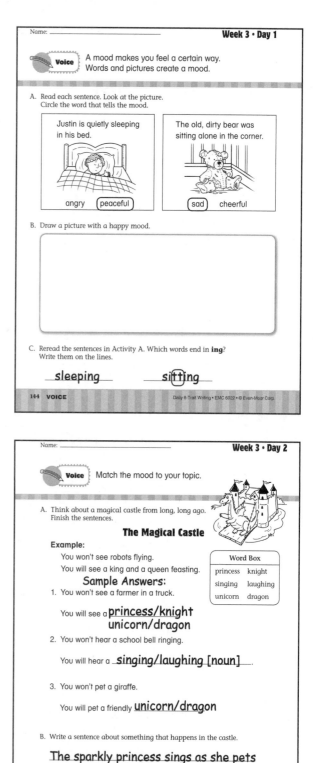

Week 3 • Day 3

Name: _____

Voice Use adjectives and verbs to create a mood.

Read each cinquain. Underline the two adjectives. Circle the three verbs ending in **ing**. Write the word from the box that best describes the mood of the poem.

Word Box
angry
fun
exciting

Piggy Bank
Round, fat
Shaking, shaking, shaking
Nothing will come out!
Money-eater

Mood: **angry**

Treasure
Shiny, gold
Hiding, digging, finding
We'll follow the map
Loot

Mood: **exciting**

Blueberry
Juicy, blue
Finding, picking, eating
Turns my teeth blue
Snack

Mood: **fun**

146   VOICE   *Daily 6-Trait Writing • EMC 6022 • © Evan-Moor Corp.*

Week 3 • Day 4

Name: _____

Voice Create a mood with a poem.

Use this chart to write a cinquain. Write about a food that is fun to eat. Create a fun mood!

Sample Answers:

marshmallows	← one word that names a food
sticky sweet	← two adjectives that describe the food
toasting melting squishing	← three verbs with **ing** that describe the food or how you eat it
glue my teeth shut	← four words that tell a feeling about the food
fluff	← another name for the food in one word

© Evan-Moor Corp. • EMC 6022 • Daily 6-Trait Writing   VOICE   147

DAY 3

Read the rule aloud and review the definitions of **adjective** and **verb**. Then say: *These kinds of words help us to create a mood. Poems are a great way to create a mood in just a few words. The poems we will read today are called cinquains. Cinquains are poems with 5 lines. They use adjectives and verbs in a pattern.* Read the poems aloud and help students understand the pattern. Then guide students through the activity.

- Read the words in the word box and the first poem aloud. Ask: *What is this poem about?* (someone trying to get money out of the bank) *How does the writer feel about the piggy bank?* (e.g., mad at it)

- Direct students to the word box. Ask: *Which of these words best describes the mood of the poem?* (angry) Then ask: *What words did the writer use to create the mood? Which words sound angry?* (e.g., repetition of **shaking**, and **nothing**, and **money-eater**) Then have students complete the activity.

DAY 4

Read the rule aloud. Use the graphic organizer to review the definition of a cinquain. Then say: *Today, we'll write a cinquain about a food that's fun to eat.*

- Guide students in brainstorming foods that are fun to eat. (e.g., watermelon, french fries, ice cream) Write students' ideas on the board.

- Draw the chart on the board and model filling it in one box at a time. For example, say: *I think that eating marshmallows is fun.* Write **marshmallows** in the first box. Then invite students to suggest words that describe marshmallows (e.g., **puffy, chewy**) and write the words in the next box. Continue with each line.

- Have students choose their own food to write about, and have them complete their poems independently.

DAY 5   *Writing Prompt*

- *Copy the cinquain you wrote on Day 4 and draw a picture that adds to the mood. Then write a sentence that tells why your food is fun to eat.*

- *Be sure words that end in ing are spelled correctly.*

Name: _____

 **Voice** A mood makes you feel a certain way.
Words and pictures create a mood.

A. Read each sentence. Look at the picture.
    Circle the word that tells the mood.

Justin is quietly sleeping in his bed.

angry   peaceful

The old, dirty bear was sitting alone in the corner.

sad   cheerful

B. Draw a picture with a happy mood.

C. Reread the sentences in Activity A. Which words end in **ing**?
    Write them on the lines.

_____   _____

Voice) Match the mood to your topic.

A. Think about a magical castle from long, long ago. Finish the sentences.

The Magical Castle

Example:

You won't see robots flying.

You will see a king and a queen feasting.

Word Box	
princess	knight
singing	laughing
unicorn	dragon

1. You won't see a farmer in a truck.

    You will see a _____.

2. You won't hear a school bell ringing.

    You will hear a _____ _____.

3. You won't pet a giraffe.

    You will pet a friendly _____.

B. Write a sentence about something that happens in the castle.

_____

_____

 **Voice**   Use adjectives and verbs to create a mood.

Read each cinquain. Underline the two adjectives.
Circle the three verbs ending in **ing**. Write the word
from the box that best describes the mood of the poem.

Word Box

angry

fun

exciting

Piggy Bank
Round, fat
Shaking, shaking, shaking
Nothing will come out!
Money-eater

Mood: _____

Treasure
Shiny, gold
Hiding, digging, finding
We'll follow the map
Loot

Mood: _____

Blueberry
Juicy, blue
Finding, picking, eating
Turns my teeth blue
Snack

Mood: _____

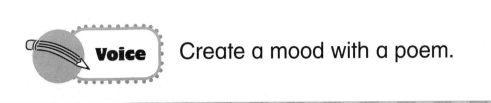 **Voice**   Create a mood with a poem.

Use this chart to write a cinquain. Write about a food that is fun
to eat. Create a fun mood!

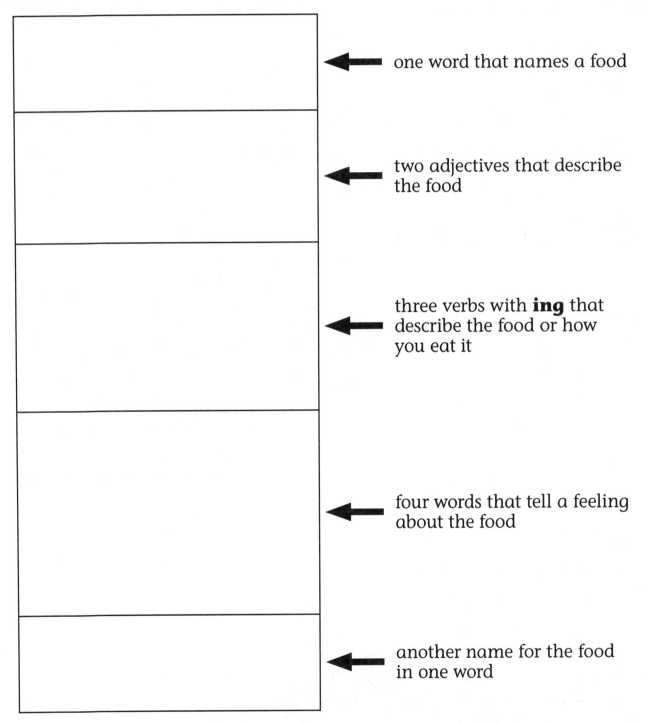

one word that names a food

two adjectives that describe
the food

three verbs with **ing** that
describe the food or how
you eat it

four words that tell a feeling
about the food

another name for the food
in one word

DAY 1

Read the rule aloud. Then say: *In a story, different characters can have different points of view. For example, in the story "Goldilocks and the Three Bears," do you think Goldilocks would tell her side of the story in the same way as the bears would tell their side?* (no) *Listen and see if you can tell whose point of view it is.* Then say: *Imagine how mad I was when I saw my porridge was gone!* (Baby Bear) *I was hungry, and there was porridge to eat.* (Goldilocks) Then guide students through the activities.

- **Activity A:** Explain that each picture tells a little story. Say: *Even though the characters in real life might not be able to speak, think about what they might say if they could.* Read aloud each sentence and have students circle the answer.

- **Activity B:** Read aloud the sentence, and ask students to imagine who or what might be talking. Have them think of several possibilities and write the one they like best.

- **Activity C:** Say: *You use an exclamation point at the end of a sentence that shows strong feeling.* Write the following sentences first without an exclamation point, then add one: *Our class is the best! I love to ride the roller coaster! Don't run into the street!* Ask: *How does the exclamation point change the sentence?* (e.g., gives it feeling; makes it stronger)

DAY 2

Read the rule aloud. Then read students the first line of this familiar nursery rhyme: *Jack and Jill went up the hill to fetch a pail of water.* Then say: *Now, what if I change it to "Jill and I went up the hill..."? Whose point of view is this?* (Jack's) Then guide students through the activities.

- **Activity A:** Have a volunteer explain what is happening in the cartoon. (A grasshopper hops on an elephant's toe.) Then read each statement and ask: *Whose point of view is this?*

- **Activity B:** Have students find the bird in the comic strip. Ask: *Whose side do you think the bird would take? Can you write in a voice that would show that the bird takes the elephant's side?* (That grasshopper was rude!) *The grasshopper's side?* (I didn't know elephants were such babies!) Then have students write their own sentences.

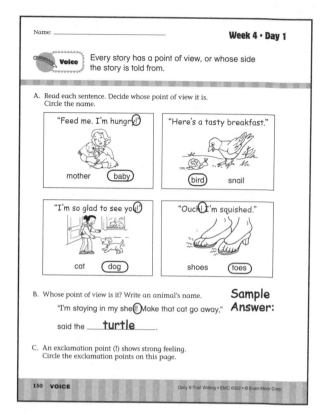

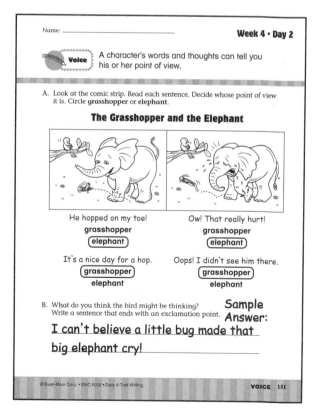

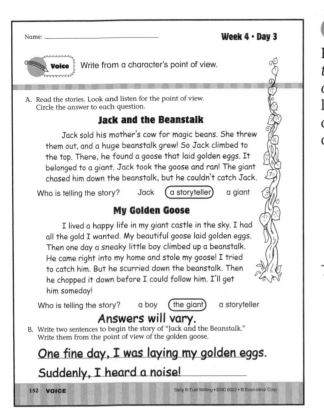

Name: _____ Week 4 · Day 3

Voice Write from a character's point of view.

A. Read the stories. Look and listen for the point of view.
Circle the answer to each question.

Jack and the Beanstalk

Jack sold his mother's cow for magic beans. She threw them out, and a huge beanstalk grew! So Jack climbed to the top. There, he found a goose that laid golden eggs. It belonged to a giant. Jack took the goose and ran! The giant chased him down the beanstalk, but he couldn't catch Jack.

Who is telling the story? Jack (a storyteller) a giant

My Golden Goose

I lived a happy life in my giant castle in the sky. I had all the gold I wanted. My beautiful goose laid golden eggs. Then one day a sneaky little boy climbed up a beanstalk. He came right into my home and stole my goose! I tried to catch him. But he scurried down the beanstalk. Then he chopped it down before I could follow him. I'll get him someday!

Who is telling the story? a boy (the giant) a storyteller

Answers will vary.

B. Write two sentences to begin the story of "Jack and the Beanstalk." Write them from the point of view of the golden goose.

One fine day, I was laying my golden eggs.

Suddenly, I heard a noise!

152 **VOICE** Daily 6-Trait Writing • EMC 6022 • © Evan-Moor Corp.

Name: _____ Week 4 · Day 4

Voice Write from different points of view.

Sample Answers:

Look at the picture story. Think about what each character might be saying or thinking. Write from each character's point of view.

Wolf: I'm coming to get you, Little Pig!

Little Pig: This boiling water will stop him!

Wolf: Help!

Little Pig: That's the end of you, Wolf!

© Evan-Moor Corp. • EMC 6022 • Daily 6-Trait Writing **VOICE** 153

DAY 3

Read the rule aloud. Then say: *Sometimes a story is told by a character. Sometimes it is told by a storyteller, or narrator, who is not part of the story.* Have students listen to these sentences from "Little Red Riding Hood" and tell if the story is told by a character or a person outside the story (storyteller):

> *I was on my way to Grandmother's house.*
> (a character, Little Red)
>
> *So I said, "Hello little girl, where are you going?"*
> (a character, the wolf)
>
> *She always wore a red riding cloak.* (storyteller)

Then guide students through the activities.

- **Activity A:** Read the first story together. Ask: *Is the story being told by a person in the story or outside?* (outside) Repeat with the second story.

- **Activity B:** Ask: *How do you think the goose felt when she was kidnapped?* (e.g., scared, surprised, mad, relieved, happy) Then have students complete the activity.

DAY 4

Read the rule aloud. Then guide students through the activities.

- Review the story of "The Three Little Pigs." Then ask: *What part of the story is shown in the pictures?* (the ending) Have students retell the ending.

- Have students brainstorm what the Wolf might be saying or thinking in the first panel. Ask: *What could you write to tell his point of view?* Continue eliciting responses for each panel.

DAY 5 *Writing Prompt*

- *Write an ending to "The Three Little Pigs." Write it from the point of view of the Wolf or one of the Pigs. Use your ideas from Day 4.*

- *Use an exclamation point to show strong feeling.*

 **Voice** Every story has a point of view, or whose side the story is told from.

A. Read each sentence. Decide whose point of view it is.
   Circle the name.

B. Whose point of view is it? Write an animal's name.

"I'm staying in my shell! Make that cat go away,"

said the _____.

C. An exclamation point (!) shows strong feeling.
   Circle the exclamation points on this page.

 **Voice**   A character's words and thoughts can tell you his or her point of view.

A. Look at the comic strip. Read each sentence. Decide whose point of view it is. Circle **grasshopper** or **elephant**.

The Grasshopper and the Elephant

He hopped on my toe!
grasshopper
elephant

Ow! That really hurt!
grasshopper
elephant

It's a nice day for a hop.
grasshopper
elephant

Oops! I didn't see him there.
grasshopper
elephant

B. What do you think the bird might be thinking?
Write a sentence that ends with an exclamation point.

_____

_____

Voice   Write from a character's point of view.

A. Read the stories. Look and listen for the point of view.
   Circle the answer to each question.

Jack and the Beanstalk

Jack sold his mother's cow for magic beans. She threw them out, and a huge beanstalk grew! So Jack climbed to the top. There, he found a goose that laid golden eggs. It belonged to a giant. Jack took the goose and ran! The giant chased him down the beanstalk, but he couldn't catch Jack.

Who is telling the story?   Jack   a storyteller   a giant

My Golden Goose

I lived a happy life in my giant castle in the sky. I had all the gold I wanted. My beautiful goose laid golden eggs. Then one day a sneaky little boy climbed up a beanstalk. He came right into my home and stole my goose! I tried to catch him. But he scurried down the beanstalk. Then he chopped it down before I could follow him. I'll get him someday!

Who is telling the story?   a boy   the giant   a storyteller

B. Write two sentences to begin the story of "Jack and the Beanstalk."
   Write them from the point of view of the golden goose.

_____

_____

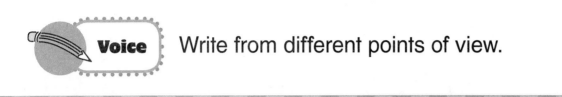

Voice   Write from different points of view.

Look at the picture story. Think about what each character might be saying or thinking. Write from each character's point of view.

Wolf: _____

_____

_____

Little Pig:_____

_____

_____

Wolf: _____

_____

_____

Little Pig:_____

_____

DAY 1

Read the rule aloud. Then review the definitions of formal and informal language. Ask: *Would you use formal or informal language in an e-mail to a friend?* (informal) *In a school report?* (formal) Then guide students through the activities.

- **Activity A:** After students complete the activity, have them give reasons to support their answers. (e.g., formal greeting; slang)

- **Activity B:** To model, write these sentences on the board: *1) This weekend, I will visit my younger sister. 2) I'm going to hang out with my little sister on Sat.* Ask: *Which of these sentences uses formal language?* (1) *Informal language?* (2) *How can you tell the difference?* (e.g., "I will visit" versus "I'm going to hang out;" **younger** versus **little**; abbreviation) Have students complete the activity.

- **Activity C (Convention):** Write the contractions **isn't** and **aren't** on the board and review how they are formed. Then say: *Some people incorrectly use the word **ain't** instead of **isn't**, **aren't**, or **am not**.* Read sentence 1 aloud and ask: *Which word could we use instead of **ain't**?* (**isn't**) Read the new sentence aloud. Have students complete the activity.

DAY 2

Read the rule aloud. Then say: *Writers can use different styles, such as serious, funny, or exciting.* Guide students through the activities.

- **Activity A:** Read the story aloud with enthusiasm and humor. Remind students to listen for the writer's style. Ask: *Who is the audience?* (children) *What writing style did the writer use?* (funny) Then discuss the lesson of the story. Ask: *What was the writer's purpose?* (to teach a lesson; to entertain) *What was the lesson?* (to be honest)

- **Activity B:** Remind students that they should use **is not** or **are not**, or their contraction forms, in place of **ain't**. Have students cross out **ain't**, write the substitute words, and find each sentence in the story to check their answers.

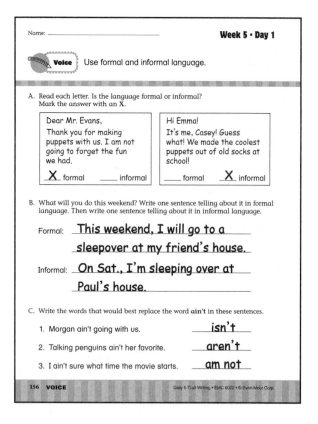

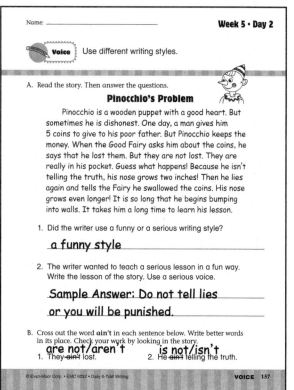

Name: _____   **Week 5 • Day 3**

Voice   Create a mood.

A. Read the story starter. Use proofreading marks to fix the use of **ain't**.

Aaron and Cho had been hiking for many hours. Then it grew dark. They heard many strange noises.

"Wooooo! Woooo!"

"That ain't an owl," whispered Aaron. isn't

"I think we should go home now. This ain't fun anymore," Cho said.

"You're right," said Aaron, looking around. "But where is home?"

B. Finish the story. Create a spooky mood.

Answers will vary.

_____
_____
_____
_____
_____
_____

158   **VOICE**   Daily 6-Trait Writing • EMC 6022 • © Evan-Moor Corp.

Name: _____   **Week 5 • Day 4**

Voice   Write from different points of view.

Think about the story of "Little Red Riding Hood."
Write what each person would say.

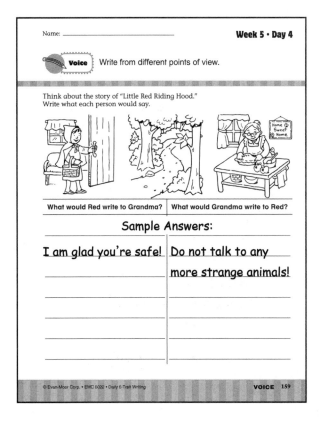

What would Red write to Grandma?	What would Grandma write to Red?
Sample Answers:	
I am glad you're safe!	Do not talk to any more strange animals!

© Evan-Moor Corp. • EMC 6022 • Daily 6-Trait Writing   **VOICE**   159

DAY 3

Read the rule aloud. Then say: **Mood** *is what adds to the overall feel of our stories.* Ask: *What kinds of moods can we create through writing?* (e.g., serious, funny, spooky, exciting, sad, angry) Then guide students through the activities.

- **Activity A (Convention):** Read the story starter aloud. Ask: *How does the story make you feel?* (e.g., scared, spooky, excited, nervous) Then direct students to find the two uses of **ain't** and replace them with better words. (**is not** or **isn't**)

- **Activity B:** Ask: *What could happen next in the story?* (e.g., they are chased through woods, they find a cabin) After students brainstorm ideas, have them write their own endings to the story. Remind them to use their unique voice to create a spooky mood.

DAY 4

Read the rule aloud. Then say: *Writers often write from different points of view. They create characters and narrators who feel differently about what happens in a story.* Review the story of "Little Red Riding Hood." Then guide students through the activity.

- Ask students to imagine that Grandmother and Red Riding Hood are writing letters to each other <u>after</u> the visit from the wolf. Brainstorm ideas from each character's point of view. Prompt students by asking: *How do you think Red Riding Hood felt after her adventure? What would she want to tell Grandmother? What would Grandmother want to tell Red Riding Hood?*

- Model writing one idea in each column. Then have students complete their own chart.

DAY 5   *Writing Prompt* ────

- *Write a letter from the point of view of Red Riding Hood or Grandmother. Use your chart from Day 4.*

- *Use **isn't, aren't**, or **am not** instead of **ain't**.*

Voice   Use formal and informal language.

A. Read each letter. Is the language formal or informal?
   Mark the answer with an **X**.

Dear Mr. Evans, Thank you for making puppets with us. I am not going to forget the fun we had. _____ formal   _____ informal

Hi Emma! It's me, Casey! Guess what! We made the coolest puppets out of old socks at school! _____ formal   _____ informal

B. What will you do this weekend? Write one sentence telling about it in formal
   language. Then write one sentence telling about it in informal language.

Formal: _____

_____

Informal: _____

_____

C. Write the words that would best replace the word **ain't** in these sentences.

1. Morgan ain't going with us.   _____

2. Talking penguins ain't her favorite.   _____

3. I ain't sure what time the movie starts. _____

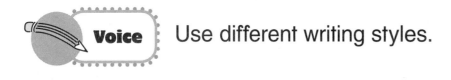

Voice   Use different writing styles.

A. Read the story. Then answer the questions.

Pinocchio's Problem

Pinocchio is a wooden puppet with a good heart. But sometimes he is dishonest. One day, a man gives him 5 coins to give to his poor father. But Pinocchio keeps the money. When the Good Fairy asks him about the coins, he says that he lost them. But they are not lost. They are really in his pocket. Guess what happens! Because he isn't telling the truth, his nose grows two inches! Then he lies again and tells the Fairy he swallowed the coins. His nose grows even longer! It is so long that he begins bumping into walls. It takes him a long time to learn his lesson.

1. Did the writer use a funny or a serious writing style?

_____

2. The writer wanted to teach a serious lesson in a fun way. Write the lesson of the story. Use a serious voice.

_____

_____

B. Cross out the word **ain't** in each sentence below. Write better words in its place. Check your work by looking in the story.

   1. They ain't lost.   2. He ain't telling the truth.

Name: ____________________

Week 5 • Day 3

Voice Create a mood.

A. Read the story starter. Use proofreading marks to fix the use of **ain't**.

Aaron and Cho had been hiking for many hours. Then it grew dark. They heard many strange noises.

"Woooo! Woooo!"

"That ain't an owl," whispered Aaron.

"I think we should go home now. This ain't fun anymore," Cho said.

"You're right," said Aaron, looking around. "But where is home?"

B. Finish the story. Create a spooky mood.

____

____

____

____

____

____

 **Voice**   Write from different points of view.

Think about the story of "Little Red Riding Hood."
Write what each person would say.

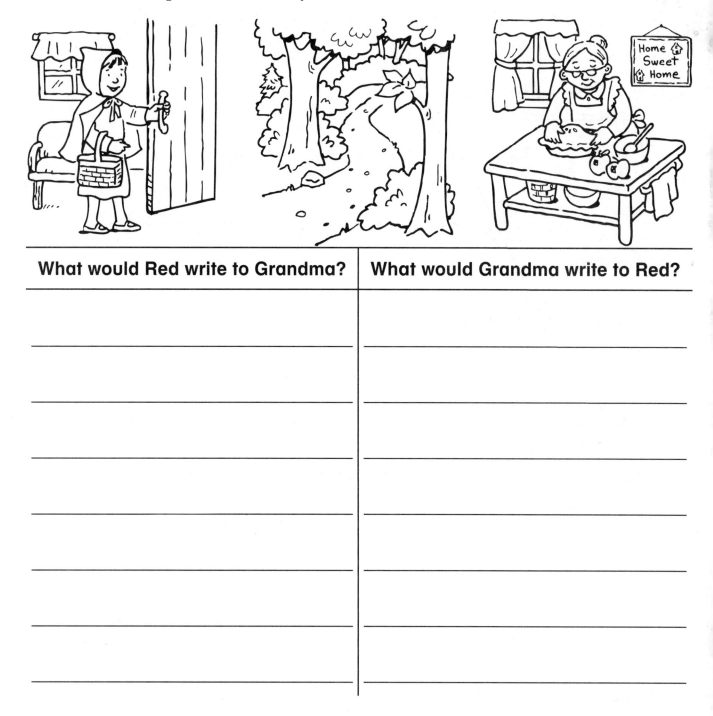

What would Red write to Grandma?	**What would Grandma write to Red?**

Proofreading Marks

Mark	Meaning	Example
℘	Take this out (delete).	I love ~~to~~ to read.
⊙	Add a period.	It was late⊙
≡	Make this a capital letter.	First prize went to maria. ≡
/	Make this a lowercase letter.	We saw a Black Cat.
___	Fix the spelling.	This is our house ~~hause~~.
⋏	Add a comma.	Goodnight⋏Mom.
˯	Add an apostrophe.	That's Lil's bike.
! ? ⋀ ⋀	Add an exclamation point or a question mark.	Help⋀Can you help me⋀
⋀	Add a word or a letter.	red The⋀pen is mine.
# ⋀	Add a space between words.	I like⋀pizza.
___	Underline the words.	We read <u>Old Yeller</u>.

Daily 6-Trait Writing • EMC 6022 • © Evan-Moor Corp.